1 MONTH OF
FREE
READING

at

www.ForgottenBooks.com

By purchasing this book you are eligible for one month membership to ForgottenBooks.com, giving you unlimited access to our entire collection of over 1,000,000 titles via our web site and mobile apps.

To claim your free month visit:

www.forgottenbooks.com/free1249326

ISBN 978-0-428-61630-4
PIBN 11249326

BIENNIAL REPORT

of the

NORTH CAROLINA STAT COMMISSION FOR THE BLIND

From July 1, 1944, through June 30, 1946

LUX ORITUR:

"And I will bring the blind by a way that they knew not;
I will lead them in paths that they have not known;
I will make darkness light before them."

—Isaiah xlii, 16.

BIENNIAL REPORT

of the

NORTH CAROLINA STATE COMMISSION FOR THE BLIND

From July 1, 1944, through June 30, 1946

LUX ORITUR:

*"And I will bring the blind by a way that they knew not;
I will lead them in paths that they have not known;
I will make darkness light before them."*

—Isaiah xlii, 16.

HONORABLE R. GREGG CHERRY
The Governor of North Carolina

"Day and night in this State of ours people use their whole minds, their full hearts, their tireless hands in meeting the responsibility of a people and a state in doing battle with the things that might hold us back and retard us.

"Based upon legislation the North Carolina State Commission for the Blind has developed a Program with the three essential cornerstones of relief, rehabilitation, and prevention of blindness. Through the development of these, the State is striving with its abundance of physical and human resources to transform lives of idleness and despondency into lives that are productive and happy and to give an equal opportunity to its visually handicapped citizens."

LETTER OF TRANSMITTAL

To Honorable R. Gregg Cherry
Governor of North Carolina
Raleigh, North Carolina

Dear Governor Cherry:

Pursuant to Chapter 53, Public Laws of 1935 and subsequent legislation, I have the honor to submit to you the accompanying report of the North Carolina State Commission for the Blind for the biennial period beginning with July 1, 1944, and ending June 30, 1946. This report concerns the management and financial transactions of this Department.

Respectfully submitted,
Sam M. Cathey, Chairman
N. C. State Commission for the Blind

MEMBERS OF THE NORTH CAROLINA STATE COMMISSION FOR THE BLIND

(Six Lay Members—Appointed by the Governor)

JUDGE SAM M. CATHEY, *Chairman*, Asheville, N. C.
DR. HOWARD E. JENSEN, *Chairman, Executive Committee*, Durham, N. C.
MR. ERNEST R. ALEXANDER, Kannapolis, N. C.
MR. V. J. ASHBAUGH, Durham, N. C.
MR. H. I. McDOUGLE, Charlotte, N. C.
MR. THOMAS S. PAYNE, Washington, N. C.

(Five Ex-Officio Members—Designated by the Legislature)

MR. R. MAYNE ALBRIGHT, *Director, State Man Power*, Raleigh, N. C.
MR. EGBERT N. PEELER, *Supt., State School for the Blind*, Raleigh, N. C.
DR. CARL V. REYNOLDS, *Secretary, State Board of Health*, Raleigh, N. C.
COL. CHARLES H. WARREN, *Supervisor, Vocational Rehabilitation,* Raleigh, N. C.
DR. ELLEN BLACK WINSTON, *State Commissioner of Public Welfare*, Raliegh, N. C.

ADVISORY MEDICAL COMMITTEE

(Surgeons certified by American Board of Ophthalmology)

DR. FRANK C. SMITH, *Chairman*, Charlotte, N. C.
DR. V. M. HICKS, *Supervising Ophthalmologist Aid to Needy Blind*, Raleigh, N. C.
DR. WM. B. ANDERSON, Durham, N. C.
DR. H. H. BRIGGS, JR., Asheville, N. C.
DR. JAMES G. JOHNSTON, Charlotte, N. C.
DR. H. C. NEBLETT, Charlotte, N. C.
DR. HENRY L. SLOAN, Charlotte, N. C.
DR. WM. S. SPEAS, Winston-Salem, N. C.
DR. S. WEIZENBLATT, Asheville, N. C.
DR. JOHN D. WILSEY, Winston-Salem, N. C.

INTRODUCTION

The laws of North Carolina place upon the North Carolina State Commission for the Blind the responsibility of motivating, administering and generally supervising a comprehensive program of activities of (1) the prevention of blindness and the restoration of sight; (2) the rehabilitation of the employable blind individual; (3) financial grants and special services to the indigent blind; and (4) employment opportunities for those who are unable to find remunerative work in private enterprises.

The purpose of this report is to present to the people of North Carolina a brief outline of the scope of the activities of one of their state agencies and its accomplishments during the biennial period of July 1, 1944—June 30, 1946. The objectives for such a program must take into account the medical, social and community aspects. During this period much emphasis has been given to co-ordinating and integrating Federal, state, local community and individual resources and directing them into channels from which the greatest good would accrue to the visually handicapped.

Each year since its establishment in 1935 the North Carolina State Commission for the Blind has grown and expanded its activities. This has been accomplished in spite of the emphasis which was given, for about four years, to winning the war; the limited number of trained persons qualified to work in so specialized a program; and marked limitations on funds.

The loyalty, perseverance and plain hard work of all persons associated with the agency and the cooperation and help given by representatives of Federal, state and local agencies as well as that received from private agencies and individuals is gratefully acknowledged.

WHEREAS I WAS BLIND, NOW I SEE

The doctors could not help. I was slowly going blind, I knew it, for the shadows were thickening, day by day; yet, deep within me, I could not accept the fact. None of my friends had ever gone blind; and it was something, as far as my experience went, which just did not, and could not happen. I had heard of blind people, had seen blind people, but knew nothing of what had caused the blindness. It was mysterious, terrible, unbelievable. It happened to other people, like the Bubonic Plague, centuries past, or to inhabitants of distant countries, but not within the bounds of my experience. I was afraid, bewildered, confused, and at times rebellious.

Then the situation changed somewhat. Part of my trouble was cataracts, but with complications; and if I waited until blindness was a reality, an operation might restore part of my vision. No one could say just how long this would take, and I could not sit for an indefinite length of time, with my hands folded, waiting for the cataracts to ripen. I now had hope; life had become a challenge. I set myself a goal to learn all I could of the ways of the visually handicapped, in order to be independent as the cataracts thickened. I determined to keep my independence. The art of finger reading and typing were soon learned as an invaluable part of my daily life. My other senses were made to function more fully, to compensate for the failing sight. Touch, taste and hearing, all were more acute, while the sense of smell became more helpful, when it, too, had to play an increasingly important part.

Two years passed, three, even ten. I had forgotten how easily and quickly small tasks could be performed with the help of sight; for I was now living as a blind person, thinking as a blind person, meeting the requirements of my environment as a blind person. This meant that it took at least three times as long to do a job well as it had in the days of sight. I was adjusted to my blindness. I had met the challenge that life had thrust upon me.

After twelve years of waiting, the day for the operation had come. What would the future now hold! I did not know, and it did not seem to matter as much now as it had during the first feverish, ignorant years.

I climbed up on the operating table, and the nurse made her preparations. I was not afraid; yet this was an important time.

I knew that much depended on my cooperation. I had confidence in my doctor, but could I depend on myself? Drops were put into my eyes, the sterile towels were adjusted, and the operation began. I was fully conscious of all that was going on around me, but of no pain, at least of none that counted. Suddenly a bright light shone before me. It had been there all the time, but it was dim to me. The doctor said a few words to his assistant, and I knew that the cataract was out. I believed that I could see once more, but I was too tired to think about it now. I wanted to sleep. I was right, the miracle was a fact, and I could now take up my life again as a sighted person.

What is it to see again? It is all the things that you might think or dream, and a great, great many more. Freedom of movement, ability to perform my daily tasks, as others did, and not self-consciously, as a blind person; to take my rightful place in a group, and not be alternately the recipient of too much or too little attention; to see facial expressions, to speak confidently, possessing as many faculties as my opponent in a discussion; to lose the inferiority complex, which came with increasing blindness. That is what my operation did for me.

Was this all? No, there were other things: to see the distant horizon, a sunset or a star, a bird's nest or the color in a red bird's wing; the smile of a friend, the blue of a baby's eyes. These joys were once more mine after the surgeon's knife had done its work.

There were prosaic little things which also gave satisfaction. The first time that I picked a pin from the floor, I had no doubt of my new-found sight. Each day, no, each hour, brings new joys and simple tasks are done with ease. The very fact of seeing now is a great diversion. During the first few weeks of restored vision, I often found myself standing before an object, a common, everyday object, like a train or a steamshovel, and gazing as if I would never get my fill. A store window was fascinating, no matter what it might contain, just as long as there were objects in it to be seen. An airplane will never lose its charm. You see, I had never seen one clearly until after the operation.

The new sight had some surprising angles. New friends, whom I had known by voice alone, were strangers when I actually saw them the first time. I had recognized them so readily before by voice. People did not look as I thought they would, nor had I always guessed correctly as to age. It was baffling, confusing.

The most unsatisfactory experience, if there could be one connected with the miracle of restored sight, was when I saw myself in the mirror, clearly and distinctly, for the first time. Do you realize what ten years can do to your face, figure, to your hair and complexion? Well, this ten year period had done all of these and more to mine, and I did not particularly like what I saw in the mirror.

These experiences I had were in part anticipated, but not the emotional reaction, which were even greater, in reverse, than those I had felt at the beginning of my handicap. The first occurred immediately after the stitches were removed, and the doctor held a strong glass before my eyes for a second. I saw clear-cut outlines of everything in front of me for the first time in ten years. The doctor says that I shrieked with delight. I don't know, but I suddenly became weak and slightly nausiated, and anxious to get back to my bed.

The Sunday after I received my new glasses, I went to church. I opened my hymn book at the place and tried to sing the words which I saw plainly on the page in front of me, but I could not sing a note. I was trembling from head to foot and had difficulty in standing to the end of the hymn. You see, for years, I could only sing those songs which I had committed to memory.

The next experience of this kind happened a few days later at a conference composed of people I knew well, but only during my handicapped days. There were special friends among them, whom I had always longed to see with my eyes, and now I had the opportunity. The words of the speaker meant little. I was too busy watching the expressions on the faces and the revealing motions of the hands of my friends. I was drunk with seeing, excited, happy, talkative. One emotion followed so quickly on the heels of another that I was exhausted at the end of each day. I was risking and jeopradizing my new gained treasure.

But now, after a period of months, the miracle of passing from shadow to sunlight, the divinely directed skill of the doctor, fill me with reverential wonder and awe. I do not regret the time spent in adjustment and learning new skills. They have enriched my life, since I am better prepared to live as a sighted person for having learned the skills of the blind. Yet this sight which has been restored to me is very precious; and I am glad that I can truthfully say in the words of the Bible, "This one thing I know, that whereas I was blind, now I see."

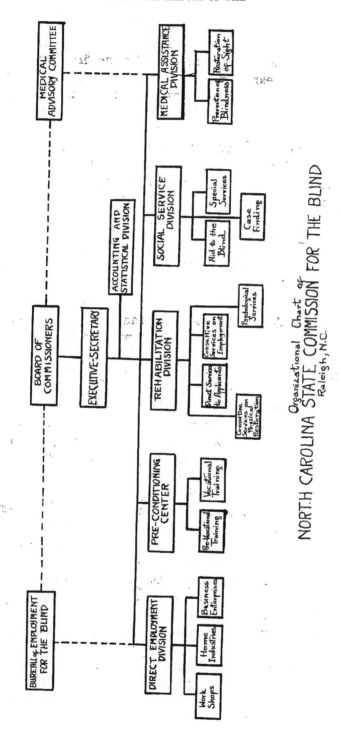

Organizational Chart of
NORTH CAROLINA STATE COMMISSION FOR THE BLIND
Raleigh, N.C.

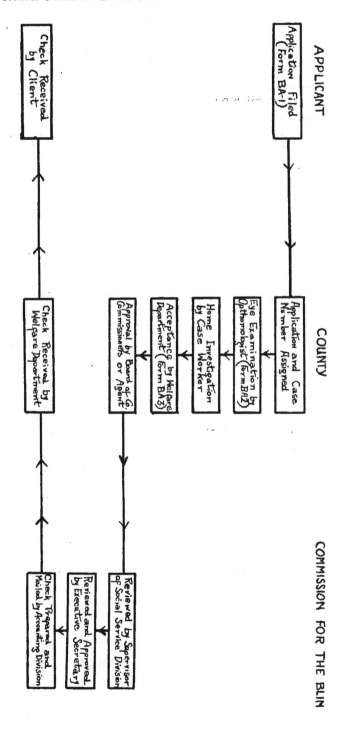

SOCIAL SERVICE DIVISION

1. Case Finding and Referral

On June 30, 1946 there were registered with the North Carolina State Commission for the Blind 7,105 individuals. On the basis of population it is estimated that there is an additional 2,500 who, during this period, were not known to the Commission. To locate these individuals and complete the register is a goal for the next biennium.

In accordance with Chapter 53, Public Laws of North Carolina 1935, Section 3, The North Carolina State Commission for the Blind maintains a currently validated census of visually handicapped individuals in the State. The census of the known blind is kept valid through the local Departments of Public Welfare, Ophthalmologists, Health Departments, school faculties, optometrists, group and continuous eye clinics—sponsored by the State Commission for the Blind, individual contacts, correspondence, Lions Clubs, Rotary, Kiwanis, Womens Clubs, Church Groups, other civic clubs and organizations et cetera. Some very interesting data about the present blind population of North Carolina will be found in appendix III.

This register of blind individuals, whether newly blinded or of longer duration, is the agency's means of interpretating to its potential clients the varied services that are available through the program of the North Carolina State Commission for the Blind. Many of these cases are persons who have become blind in adult life are financially independent but are in need of occupational therapy; instructions in reading and writing Braille; typewriting; signature writing; family adjustment to blindness; adjustment to travel; recreation; instruction in family and individual budgeting; interpretation of available eye care and physical care and follow-up of physicians recommendations. Those who are in need of financial assistance and/or are eligible for rehabilitation services are referred to the proper division for services.

2. Aid to the Blind

To the many complicated problems that blindness brings there is often added other physical disabilities which have resulted from the same injury, disease, or condition that caused blindness thus rendering the individual unemployable and dependent upon his government for the necessities of life. The loss of vision should not prohibit an individual from the participation in every activity enjoyed by the person with vision. The blind individual has the right to work, the right to equal pay, the right to uniform security and the right to legal safeguards. It is the latter two of these four rights that we are particularly concerned in the establishing of eligibility for Blind Aid.

During the past biennium 2,372 blind persons received blind assistance on the basis of economic need. This assistance has been made possible through Title X of the Social Security Act of 1935, amended in 1939, in cooperation with State Law of 1937 and subsequent laws which were enacted for the purpose of enabling this State Agency to furnish financial assistance to its needy individuals. To be eligible to receive Blind Aid in North Carolina a person must have resided in North Carolina for one year immediately preceding the date of application, is not receiving Old Age Assistance, is not living in a Public Institution or will not live in a Public Institution after receipt of grant, does not have sufficient income to meet his economic need, is not publicly soliciting alms and certifies through his signature that the information which he has given in proving his eligibility is correct. The program for Aid to the Blind is administered locally by the County Departments of Public Welfare as the local agents of the Board of County Commissioners and the North Carolina State Commission for the Blind. Blind persons receiving this assistance are those individuals whom the Commission has been unable to assist in becoming self-supporting and who have no relatives who are able to provide the minimum necessities of life. The majority of these individuals have some other handicap in addition to blindness such as advanced age, poor health, or other disabilities and can never become employable. The average monthly grant during the biennium per blind recipient was $18.78 which is $9.74 less than the National average of $28.52 per month per individual. North Carolina is eight from the bottom.

There are pending at the present time 1,073 needy blind persons who are eligible under the law for Aid to the Blind but who cannot be aided because of insufficient state funds to assist them. The majority of these individuals who are pending in the files of the State Commission for the Blind, as in the case of the present recipients, include blind people who have other major physical handicaps in addition to blindness.

Because of depletion of State Aid to the Blind funds, the State Commission for the Blind has had to reject requests for increased Blind Aid grants to individuals whose increased need was brought about through the increased cost of living and the extreme shortage of housing facilities for blind persons. Many County Departments of Public Welfare, through their County Boards of Public Welfare and Boards of County Commissioners, have requested that state funds be set up this fiscal year to match the increased County funds that could be made available; which plan was rejected by the State Commission for the Blind based on insufficient state funds.

An application for Aid to the Blind is made in the local Department of Public Welfare by the applicant in person, by members of family, or by a friend who knows the financial need of the applicant. (See flow chart of applications and payment of Aid to the Blind grants on page 11.)

At this time the applicant is given a Physician's Report of Eye Examination, Form BA-2, to be presented to the Ophthalmologist on which is recorded the vision of the individual with and without glasses. This is proof of the eligibility requirement of blindness. The Special Case Worker for the Blind in the local Department of Public Welfare makes a home investigation, and with the applicant, completes the application for Blind Aid. All application forms completely filled in, together with the Case Worker's recommendation, and Form BA-3 requesting decision of the Superintendent of Public Welfare are referred to the County Superintendent of Public Welfare. The Superintendnt makes his decision, signs the forms BA-1 and BA-3. The completed application is then presented to the Board of County Commissioners by the Superintendent of Public Welfare in applicant's county of legal residence for their decision. After both decisions are made, the application is prepared and mailed by the County Department of Public Welfare to the State Commission for the Blind where it is reviewed by the Supervisor of the Social Service Division and together with her recommendation the application is reviewed and approved by the Executive Secretary of the State Commission for the Blind. All applications are processed in the Accounting Division of the Commission and a check is written for the applicant whose application has been approved. All Aid to the Blind checks are mailed on the last day of the preceding month to the County Department of Public Welfare to be delivered to the Blind Aid recipients.

Under Title X of the Federal Social Security Act, the Social Security Board pays one-half of the Aid to the Blind grants now being given to needy blind and allows, in addition, one-half of the cost of the administration of the aid to the blind program. The Social Security Board also supervises the Aid to the Blind program.

The following data on blind persons who have received direct aid during the period from July 1, 1944, through June 30, 1946 presents some very interesting facts.

SOCIAL DATA ON CURRENT RECIPIENTS OF AID TO THE BLIND ON CASES CLOSED AND ON APPLICANTS REJECTED FROM JULY 1, 1944 THROUGH JUNE 30, 1946

1. Average number blind persons receiving direct monthly
aid during period 2,372

2. Number Blind North Carolina Citizens Eligible Under
Law to Receive but Appropriations are Inadequate   .   . 1,073

3. Number applications denied blind aid 151
   Reasons aid denied:
   Ineligible because of too much vision 46
   Ineligible because of residence requirements ..   . 2
   Eligible for other form of assistance 7
   Inmates of Public Institution   5
   Other resources 76
   Other 15

4. Number blind persons whose cases were closed 659
   Reasons:
   Vision wholly or partially restored 53
   Death 317
   Moved out of state   ..:... 16
   Became self-supporting 69
   Receipt of allotment or allowance of men in armed
   forces 40
   Supported by income from relatives   95
   Admitted to public institution 56
   Other 13

5. National Average Monthly Grant Per Blind Recipient . .. $28.52

6. North Carolina's Average Monthly Grant Per Blind Recipient $18.78

7. Average range of individual monthly grants during
   period:
   $ 7.00-$ 9.99 65
   10.00- 14.99 651
   15.00- 19.99 723
   20.00- 24.99 412
   25.00- 29.99 219
   30.00- 40.00 302

8. Age of blind persons receiving direct aid:
    0-14 years' 10
    15-24 years 116
    25-54 years 809
    55 and over 1,437
9. Race of blind persons receiving direct aid:
    White 1,283
    Colored   1,057
    Indian 32

3. Talking Book Machines

As in previous years, the State Commission for the Blind has continued the service of loaning Talking Book Machines to the blind in the State of North Carolina. The close of this year found 171 machines distributed to blind individuals throughout the State during the Biennium ending June 30, 1946. These machines are distributed by the State Commission for the Blind through the courtesy of the Library of Congress, Washington, D. C.

The County Department of Public Welfare, through its Special Case Worker for the Blind and the field staff of the State Commission for the Blind, accepts applications from individuals, approves them if found eligible and mails them to the State Commission for the Blind. These applications are reviewed and if approved, the machines are delivered when available. The loan, delivery and servicing of these machines is done without any charge whatever to the blind individual. If a machine needs adjustment or repair it is sent directly to the State Commission for the Blind where it is prepared for shipment to the American Foundation for the Blind Repair Department. These machines are of two types, the spring driven type that may be used where electricity is not available and the electric type.

Records can be obtained directly from the Library of Congress by the owner of the machine. Books of interesting variety, including the Bible, books on travel, fiction, biography and history are available.

Quite often the blind individual does not understand the wide use that may be made of the Talking Book Machine or how it may be operated by the blind individual. The Special Case Worker is very helpful in the demonstration of it.

Because of shortage of materials needed in the manufacture of parts and the new machines, it has been difficult for the State Commission for the Blind in North Carolina to supply the demand.

4. Special Services

In approximately one-third of the Counties of North Carolina, Special Case Workers for the Blind are employed on a part-time basis by the Lions Club or the County Association for the Blind or a Woman's Club to render special services to the blind individuals who are not necessarily in need of financial assistance.

The main objective of these special services are, (1.) To assist the individual in making the psychological adjustment to his handicap; (2.) To assist the family group in adjusting to the blind member; (3.) To assist the blind individual to become a participating member of society. To accomplish these aims, the following techniques and methods are used by the Special Case Worker:

1. Academic Instruction: There have been 1,040 visits made by the Special Case Workers for the Blind in giving special instructions in reading and writing Braille, moon type or New York point; typewriting and signature writing, explaining the

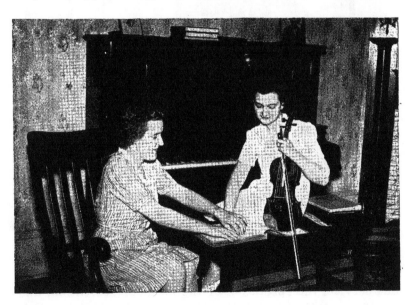

The use of braille music in learning to play the piano is one of the special services offered to blind individuals.

use, care, and taking applications for talking books; also in explaining the availability of Braille magazines. Even though a person has had the best educational advantages, blindness brings with its many other deprivations, illiteracy, as the individual must learn again to read and write.

2. Assistance in Family Adjustment: There have been 2,048 visits made in the homes of blind individuals by the special Case Workers for the Blind to instruct the family in ways of helping the blind person. If he can be made employable, his abilities are discussed with him and he is assisted in developing them. Many blind people cannot become efficient enough in industrial work to earn a living, but may be able to once again share in the responsibilities of the home and to become a contributing citizen in the community in which he lives. During these visits, assistance is given through interpretation of the need of the blind member and the ways in which the family may assist this member in adjustment to blindness through arrangement of furniture, use of

Young blind mother learning to care for her child as taught by Special Case Worker.

guide service, interpretation of the need for recreation, and the type of recreation in which a blind member may participate, the need for exercise and fresh air, assistance in focusing the attention of the family on the care of the health; the need for participation of the blind member in community life; assisting the family in a better understanding of the effect of blindness to reduce fear and negative emotional reactions.

3. Assistance in the Personal Adjustment of Blindness: There have been 2,373 visits made during the past Biennium in assisting the individual to regain his normal place in the family circle through instruction in doing things without vision formerly done and to assume his obligations and responsibilities in the home, neighborhood and community. This assistance was extended to persons in order that they may develop to a maximum degree their other senses and rely more effectively upon their power of memory and the remaining senses, employability, personal appearance, care of clothing, and personal toiletry; ways and means of avoiding blindisms and the cultivation of facial animation, habits of the seeing person, and looking directly at the person to whom the individual is speaking; better understanding of acceptable eating habits is tactfully thought through. Through this service, the Special Case Worker for the Blind teaches recreation and handling of money, instructions in social conventions, in obstacle awareness, and manual dexterity. Many individuals need instructions in methods of exercising the fingers to make them more sensitive and nimble on the tips. In facing reality situations the Special Case Worker for the Blind is able to instill courage and expanded interests in additional activities, to interpret to individuals their own reactions, and to assist the individual

This person with a major handicap in addition to blindness supplements his income through home industries.

in reducing fear. In meeting the normal drives, affection, recognition, adventure and accomplishment, a cooperative selection is made from therapy crafts and hobby crafts and adjustment to travel. He is given instructions in the use of travel aids, such as the white cane and public conveyances. During the past biennium 5,537 visits have been made in the homes of the adult blind in teaching some type of hobby crafts or therapy crafts, such as, cooking, weaving, sewing, chair bottoming, mat making, leather work, basketry, crocheting, knitting, gardening, etc. As illustrated in the photographs on special services to the blind, the value of some of these services in child care, therapy crafts, and in Braille music are illustrated. The visits as noted above are visits which have included less than one-third of the blind population of North Carolina. Demand for these services through the North Carolina State Commission for the Blind during a biennium are enormous for persons who are not in economic need but are in need of only specialized services. The following is an excerpt from a recent letter, "I am the wife of a prominent lawyer and am gradually losing my vision through diseased optic nerves. My husband is willing to read to me but I have a desire to learn Braille and read for myself. Is there any service which you could render?" Because of this demand we are requesting additional funds to help these persons in their homes in the specialized services which the special Case Worker for the Blind in the Welfare Departments in North Carolina is equipped to offer.

A SURVEY OF THE RESOURCES AND ACCOMPLISHMENTS OF THE MEDICAL DIVISION

A medical eye care program in a public agency includes prevention of blindness, conservation and restoration of vision. This is best achieved by close cooperation with all organized community resources and an informed public. "Why did I not know?" was the question of a grief-stricken woman who had lost her vision from glaucoma or hardening of the eye ball. "Why had not someone told me that I needed periodic eye examinations by a qualified ophthalmologist?" This person might have obtained useful vision all of her life by continued treatment by an eye physician. "Why did I not have periodic physical examinations?" was the desperate question asked by a diabetic patient who had lost her vision because of an untreated physical condition.

Through the combined efforts of the State Commission for the Blind, the County Health and Welfare Departments, other public and private agencies and Lions and other civic clubs during this biennial period, vision has been restored to 1163 persons and blindness has been prevented for countless others.

The Health Departments have done notable work in prevention of blindness through control of infectious diseases and sponsoring of eye clinics. In counties where there are no Health Departments the Welfare Departments sponsor eye clinics, and in some counties both serve as co-sponsors. Through the cooperation of both agencies The Commission for the Blind has held 287 clinics during this period in which 7,174 examinations were made. A total of 1,483 were recipients of medical eye service.

Examinations made by an apthalmologist and proper fitting of glasses by an optician are provided for in the clinics conducted for the purpose of preventing blindness.

The County Welfare Departments determine eligibility for medical eye care on the basis of financial need and refer the applicants to the State Commission for the Blind for available services.

Two sight-saving classes were organized in the fall of 1945, and work has been done toward the end of establishing at least two more in schools in the larger urban centers. The two new classes, added to the one established in 1936, make a total of

Large type print, special lighting and scientifically adapted equipment reduce eye strain in sight-saving classes.

three in the State. Children benefitted by these classes are those whose vision is too defective to function as a sighted person, yet have some useful vision which disqualifies them for enrollment in the School for the Blind. Conservative estimates have led us to expect to find one of each five hundred of the school population in need of sight-saving class services. Large-type print is used, scientific lighting, with special attention to the prevention of glare, and all other means possible to give the minimum eye strain to school work. Talking Books help in lesson preparation, which is supplemented by the teacher's reading aloud. Typewriters save eye strain necessary in writing by hand. Specially-built desks help in adjusting to maximum lighting.

A medical center located in Charlotte, North Carolina renders services on an area basis. Appointments are given for eye examinations, refractions, and eye surgery. Through the cooperation of the Variety Club, the services of the physicians and the State

Handicrafts are important activities in sight-saving classes.

Commission for the Blind, the clinic is maintained. The Health and Welfare Departments from 10 to 12 counties use the clinic for their clients. Doctors in the surrounding counties send cases in for consultation, surgery and treatment. One colored and four white doctors participate in the medical activities of the center. Through this center 1048 persons received medical eye services during this biennial period.

Other services are offered the counties without physicians. Periodically during a year an eye physician and a Medical Social Worker of the Commission staff go into rural counties to hold eye examination clinics. These are held at the request of Health and Welfare Departments. New blind cases are found through these clinics and offered all services which the Commission is prepared to give: surgery for the restoration and conservation of vision or prevention of blindness, and surgery for cosmetic effect. Enrollment in the School for the Blind is explained by the Medical Social Worker to parents of blind children; and blindness is reported to the Department of Public Welfare, and, in case of children, to the State School for the Blind. Eligibility for Aid to the Blind on the basis of vision is determined, and eye reports signed by the physician are left in the Welfare Department. Clients are informed of rehabilitation services available to them either through our agency or through the Rehabilitation Division of the Education Department. Eye conditions are explained to clients by the physician, and surgery recommended by the physician is offered to the indigent clients without cost to them.

Surgery is done in several Medical Centers where hospitals and qualified ophthalmologists are located. As often as possible, clients are given the doctor of their choice. The doctors have been generous with their time during the war years when their private practice was almost too heavy to carry. They have marked off blocks of time from their private appointment books to give time needed to carry on work for the indigent visually handicapped and blind people. Their skill has alleviated suffering, restored vision, and prevented blindness. The hospitals have cooperated by allocating a number of beds for eye work. Beds have been limited, however, and applicants are waiting who need surgery and treatment. The Superintendent of the State School for the Blind has demonstrated his interest and cooperation by lending the School Infirmary for a surgical and treatment center for several weeks during the summer.

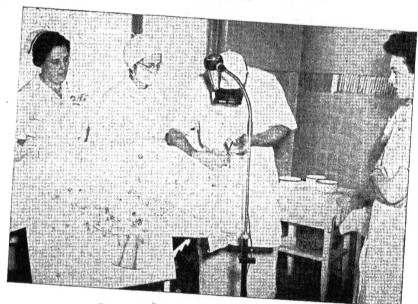

Restoration of sight through surgery.

New Goals

We look forward to new goals in prevention, conservation and restoration of vision. We need to study new and changing causes of blindness. By improved methods of treatment of veneral diseases, we expect less blindness from these causes. Better protection from injury from accidents in industry, a better understanding by individuals everywhere of the relation of a healthy body to good eye sight, and of the importance of periodic eye, and physical examinations by qualified physicians, are desirable. More attention should be paid to the eyes of pre-school children with evidence of defective vision and to the eyes of elderly groups. More public education in eye hygiene is needed. We believe that every person asking for our service has a right to good medical eye care. A better understanding of resources available and causes of blindness and defective vision, we believe, will enable each community to secure better service in prevention of blindness.

The 8-year-old child shown above was deaf, dumb and blind before her sight was restored through surgery.

VOCATIONAL REHABILITATION

"My share of the work of the world may be limited, but the fact that it is work makes it precious.

There is no doubt in my mind that we render the greatest service to the unfortunate when we enable them to feel that they are useful members of society, capable of working for others as well as for themselves."—Helen Keller.

"Rehabilitation means rebuilding, retraining and returning a handicapped individual to remunerative employment and his rightful place in the society of mankind. Rehabilitation looks at the Man and not his Disability. On this premise the processes of Rehabilitation Service to the Blind and Visually Handicapped proceed. Vocational rehabilitation has been compared to the task of a production engineer—finding and bringing together materials and services to build socially and economically independent units from human wrecks.' "—H. B. Cummings.

It was not until the end of World War I that any attention was given to the many handicapped persons which comprise our population. At first the civilian had no part nor consideration in the plan for rehabilitation services, only War Disabled persons. Slowly through the years cognizance was taken of the many other disabled persons, who could become self-maintaining if only given a chance—finding the person, restoring health, retraining and placing in employment. In 1943 the Congress of the United States not only recognized but made provision for both veterans and civilians prevented from work by various handicaps. North Carolina's own Congressman, Graham Barden, was co-author of the Barden-LaFollette Bill which was enacted by Congress July 1943.

With the enlargement of services that could be rendered, both physical and mental restoration, towards employment, and an increase in funds by the Federal Government and the necessary Legislation in our own State, the present status of Rehabilitation was achieved.

Vocational Rehabilitation involves certain processes, the most important of these are:

Case finding
Counselling and Guidance
Training
Placement
Post Placement Supervision

1. *Case Finding:* All the services available to the visually handicapped cannot be rendered until the person has been found. This is the first job of the Rehabilitation Department to find the individual so that he may accept or reject the services that can be offered to each handicapped person in the State. There are too many persons who have not found the Rehabilitation Department nor has the Department found them. This, then, is where the Rehabilitation Department of the Commission as well as the

whole Commission is placing its energy and effort. After a person is found, he must be interviewed to see if he has rehabilitation qualifications. Rehabilitation looks at the Total Man—in the light of employability considering these characteristics: physical ability to work, mental and educational ability to learn and to hold a job, personality equal to employment and skill in a job or ability to render service which someone is willing to buy.

2. *Counselling and Guidance:* The aim of vocational counselling is to help the client in his choice of a suitable employment objective, in planning his preparation for such employment, and in achieving those attitudes which will bring success and satisfaction in his job. Counselling is based on an understanding of the "whole" individual with due regard to individual differences which exist in all persons in the world, and the fact that the client is the one to be served. It is he who is to be made self-maintaining by the processes of Rehabilitation. Every effort must be expended to remove or attempt to remove the handicap. Physical restoration is the first step after a client has been accepted by the counselor for rehabilitation services, not only physical restoration but mental restoration or improvement is given due consideration.

The role of a counselor in Rehabilitation is the most important —he is dealing with a human life, he is having a part in the plans of a human—only counselors skilled in the techniques of such an art should be entrusted with so great a task.

3. *Training:* On the completion of a plan and objective for rehabilitation, the third large step is the training program. This may take many channels, such as training for stand operation, in the workshop, in industry and in colleges and universities. The Counselor is responsible for the type and quality of training rendered. He should keep constant watch to see that the client is receiving the kind of training which will fit him for remunerative employment. Eventual employment is the motivation of the Rehabilitation Department.

4. *Placement:* All the above mentioned processes in Rehabilitation must lead to the goal of placement in a job, occupation or profession; job placement which will allow the handicapped individual to use all his abilities and develop his capabilities.

In the dark ages of civilization, the only "job" a blind person could work at was that of a mendicant. Through the years of hu-

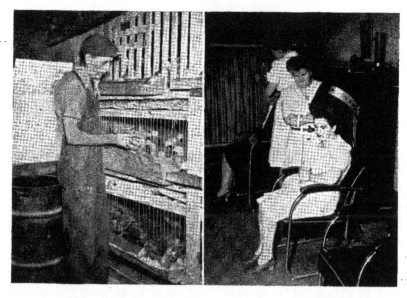

This blind man has been made self-supporting through raising poultry.

This blind woman operates successfully her own beauty parlor.

man progress, development and interpretation, it has been conclusively proven that blind persons do not want to beg, that begging is an insult to any self-respecting blind person. Gradually over the latter years, it has been conceded that a blind person could successfully manage and operate concession stands or small businesses. With these two hurdles out of the way and a platform to use as a springboard to greater opportunities, the Rehabilitation Department is attempting to open up new jobs, new professions and semi-professional employment. Much effort and energy has been expended on this phase of the program. The surface has only been scratched and the search for different types of placement will be continued and emphasized.

With the view of bringing to the blind heretofore unexplored professional employment, the Rehabilitation Department of the State Commission for the Blind has conducted a nation-wide survey of professions in which the blind of the nation are engaged. There are now 20 different types of professional men and women in North Carolina. Some of these openings in employment are in these fields: law, social work, teachers, osteopaths, chiropractors, masseurs, hydrotherapy, music teachers, orchestra leaders, instrumentalists, vocalists, ministers, including directors of church music, radio announcers and various other fields. The nation-wide survey of professional placements disclosed that much research must be done along this line if the blind of our nation and especially our own state are to be offered jobs equal to their abilities. This project will be continued during the years to come. Many placements of the Rehabilitation Department are made through the Bureau of Employment for the blind in stands and businesses under the central control system. The Bureau offers excellent opportunities of employment of the blind and visually handicapped.

Since blind persons have as diverse personalities and environments as the general population, it has been found necessary to use a variety of placements to adapt employment to the individuals. The Rehabilitation Counselor arranges for and supervises such placements. There are blind people successfully employed in the following jobs: Rural stores, telephone exchange operators, fix-it-shops, florist shops, music stores, knitting mills, cement block business, print shops, grist mills, dry cleaning business, motion picture operator, and many other jobs and occupations.

5. *Post Placement Supervision:* The last of the major steps in the rehabilitation processes is Post Placement Supervision.

Through the services of the Rehabilitation Division the radio announcer (left) and the minister of music (right) are now self-supporting.

Grocery store (left) and print shop (right) are fields in which blind people find opportunities for successful rehabilitation.

After a person is placed, he needs guidance and supervision to some degree to insure steady progress. The rehabilitation coun-selors visit the blind person at regular intervals as long as this is needed for continued success and development. With noted progress in the management of his job, the counselor visits at less frequent intervals or when he is called upon by his former client. Post Placement Supervision continues as long as the client operates or performs on the job. The aim of rehabilitation is not only to set one blind person up in a job, but also to find new job opportunities for the blind.

The succeeding tables show the progress made in the Rehabil-itation Department during the past biennium in placing persons in gainful employment. The total number of persons placed is 333, in 67 different types of work with an average weekly wage of $27.18. If the dignity of the individual is forgotten and only the cost to the tax payer considered, these 333 persons on relief would have cost the county, state and Federal Government $87,-912.00 and only a small part of their needs have been met in this manner. From these figures it would appear that rehabilitation services pay very high dividends in both human conservation and financial expenses.

The second table carries the various types of placements which the Commission has made since it began functioning in 1936. There are 110 types of employment listed as engaged in by the blind of North Carolina.

Under the enlarged program, rehabilitation services to the blind and visually handicapped is just beginning to broaden and develop. In the coming biennium new vistas of employment will be explored, new opportunities offered—the goal of the department is to assist through our services, every visually handicapped person in North Carolina capable of employment, to achieve job satisfaction and regain and maintain his place in the society of mankind—to fulfill the mission of mankind on earth—work.

Under the Barden Rehabilitation Act, the Vocational Rehabilitation Division of the Federal Security Agency pays one-half of the rehabilitation case service costs of physical restoration, training, placement, etc., for blind people who are considered to be employable and all of the costs of rehabilitation office administration, vocational guidance and placement staff, and of war disabled civilians. The Federal Vocational Rehabilitation Division supervises the rehabilitation program for the blind and serves as an office of clearance and exchange of new and successful ideas and methods of rehabilitation for the forty-eight states.

The operation of music stores offers interesting employment for blind people.

Table I—Data on 333 blind persons aided in employment during past biennium

Occupation or Business Operated	Number of Persons			Average Weekly Earnings**
	Total	Male	Female	
* TOTAL	333	237	96	$27.18
Bakery Employees	3	3		18.50
Barbecue Place Owners	1	1		30.00
Beauty Parlor Owners	2		2	30.00
Boat Rental Service	1	1		30.00
Cafe Owners	1	1		45.00
Candy Wrappers	1		1	19.75
Cement Block Makers	1	1		45.00
Clerks	3	3		28.25
Clothing Store Owners	1	1		50.00
Combers	1	1		25.00
Concession Stand Operators	67	40	27	21.34
Corn Graders	1	1		16.25
Dairy Hands	2	2		24.00
Delivery Boys	1	1		15.00
Dietitians	1		1	35.00
Domestic Servants	2		2	12.50
Dry Cleaning Business	1	1		35.00
Electricians	1	1		35.00
Farmers	15	13	2	14.00
Filling Station Workers	3	3		23.75
Fishermen	1	1		12.00
Furniture Manufacturers	1	1		50.00
Furniture Store Owners	1	1		50.00
Grocery Store Merchants	43	38	5	21.18
Housekeepers	7	1	6	14.58
Industrial Workers	13	11	2	27.69
Janitors	3	3		12.62
Junk Dealers	1	1		20.00
Laborers	8	8		19.20
Lappers	1	1		26.20
Laundry Workers	1	1		16.00
Lawyers	1	1		63.00
Maintenance Men	1	1		18.00
Masseurs	7	5	2	21.56
Mattress Businesses	13	12	1	26.21
Musicians	2	2		35.00
Newsboys	1	1		10.00
Novelty Shop Owners	1		1	20.00
Packers	15	10	5	20.00
Peanut Vendors	1	1		6.00
Photographers	1	1		25.00
Piano Retailers	2	2		50.00
Piano Tuners	11	11		32.92
Plumbers	1	1		18.00
Poultry Farmers	4	4		13.50
Printers	1	1		30.00
Quill Skinners	1	1		26.20
Radio Engineers	1	1		31.25
Radio Retailers	1	1		22.50

Occupation or Business Operated	Number of Persons			Average Weekly Earnings**
	Total	Male	Female	
Recreational Directors	1	1		37.50
Rope Splicing	1		1	15.00
Salesmen, Salesladies	3	2	1	23.25
Saw Mill Workers	2	2		18.00
Seamstresses	6		6	17.71
Secretaries, Typists	3		3	23.34
Shipping Helpers	1	1		30.00
Social Workers	9		9	34.00
Soda Shops	3	3		21.00
Spoolers	2		2	22.25
Teachers	6	4	2	27.72
Telephone Exchange Operators	1	1		30.00
Textile Workers	5	5		29.75
Theatre Projectionists	1	1		30.00
Ticket Agents	3	3		30.00
Workshop Employees	31	17	14	15.07

* This total represents the number of persons assisted during the biennium, and not the number of placements made. Some persons have been placed several times in the process of finding suitable employment for the induvidual.

** This figure indicates average weekly earnings at the time of placement and does not show increments.

Table II—Data on 1023 blind persons aided in employment since 1936

Occupation or Business Operated	Number of Persons			Avargge Weekly Earnings**
	Total	Male	Female	
* TOTAL	1023	759	264	$26.85
Bakery Employees.	3	3		18.50
Barbecue Stand Owners.	1	1		30.00
Beauty Parlor Operators.	1		1	30.00
Beauty Parlor Owners	2		2	30.00
Barber Shops	1	1		{ 7.00
Boarding House Operator.	3		3	12.00
Boat Rental Service.	1	1		30.00
Bookeepers.	1	1		50.00
Cabinet Makers.	1	1		16.00
Caddy.	1	1		10.00
Cafe Operators.	3	3		20.00
Cafe Owners.	1	1		45.00
Candy and Sandwich Wrappers.	7	4	3	18.42
Casket Finishers.	1	1		35.00
Cement Block Business	2	2		40.00
Chair Caners.	4	4		7.25
Clerks.	3	3		28.25
Clothing Store Operators.	2	2		32.50
Coal Dealers.	3	3		35.00
Combers.	1	1		25.00
Concession Stand Operators.	177	119	58	20.00
Construction Workers.	12	12		13.17
Corn Graders.	1	1		16.25
Dairy Hands.	4	4		20.00
Defense Workers.	2	2		37.40
Delivery Boys.	1	1		15.00
Dietitians.	1		1	35.00
Domestic Servants	2		2	12.50
Dry Cleaning Business.	2	2		32.50
Electricians.	2	2		45.00
Farm Agents.	1	1		35.00
Farmers.	45	43	2	13.00
Filling Station Opeators.	10	10		26.65
Fishermen.	1	1		12.00
Fish Market Owners.	1	1		8.00
Fix-it Shops	2	2		40.00
Floor Sanders.	1	1		14.00
Florists.	2	2		21.00
Furniture Finishers.	2	2		25.00
Furniture Manufacturers.	1	1		50.00
Furniture Store Owners	2	2		35.00
Gardners.	1	1		11.50
Grist Mill Operators.	4	4		17.00
Grocery Store Operators.	113	96	17	16.50
Handicrafts and Needle Work.	2	1	1	8.50
Health Department Helpers.	2	2		25.00
Housekeepers.	7	1	6	14.58
Industrial Workers.	13	11	2	27.69
Janitors.	5	5		15.00
Junk Dealers	1	1		20.00
Justice of Peace.	1	1		8.00.
Laborers.	19	17	2	15.30
Lappers.	1	1		26.20
Laundry Workers.	4	4		12.00
Lawyers	5	5		45.65

Occupation or Business Operated	Number of Persons			Average Weekly Earnings**
	Total	Male	Female	
Looper Clip Project	8	4	4	$ 7.00
Lumber Industry	5	5		19.63
Maintenance Men	1	1		18.00
Messeurs	12	10	2	24.00
Mattress Business	32	31	1	25.00
Meat Cutters	1	1		25.00
Mechanics	2	2		17.50
Mica Guaging	41	17	24	16.00
Musicians	6	6		25.00
News Butch	1	1		125.00
Newsboys	3	3		12.00
Night Clerks	1	1		25.00
Night Watchman	1	1		21.00
Novelty Shop Owners	1		1	20.00
Osteopathic Physicians	1	1		35.00
Packers	20	14	6	20.50
Painters	1	1		36.00
Peanut Vendors	4	4		10.00
Pharmacists	1	1		30.00
Photography	2	2		25.00
Piano Retailers	6	6		45.00
Piano Tuners	37	37		30.00
Plumbers	3	3		22.00
Pool Table Chain Operators	2	2		27.50
Poultry Raisers	12	9	3	13.00
Preachers	4	4		25.00
Printers	1	1		30.00
Produce Dealers	1	1		15.00
Quill Skinners	2	2		26.20
Radio Announcers	2	2		26.55
Radio Engineers	1	1		31.25
Radio Retailers	1	1		22.50
Recreational Directors	1	1		37.50
Rope Splicing	1		1	15.00
Salesmen, Saleswomen	14	9	5	19.22
Saw Mill Workers	2	2		18.00
Seamstresses	6		6	17.71
Secretaries, Typists	8	1	7	25.00
Shoe Store Operators	1	1		15.00
Shipping Clerks	2	2		26.50
Ship Yard Workers	1	1		35.00
Social Workers	42	7	35	35.00
Soda Shops	6	6		37.50
Spoolers	2	2		22.25
Sweepers	1	1		18.00
Teachers	22	9	13	25.00
Telephone Exchange Operators	4	4		25.00
Textile Workers	17	15	2	22.00
Theatre Projectionists	1	1		30.00
Ticket Agents	3	3		30.00
Time Keepers	1	1		30.00
Tire Recappers	2	2		22.50
Tobacco Factory Workers	1	1		16.00
Truckers	2	2		21.25
Tutors	3	2	1	11.25
Workshop Employees	172	113	59	15.00

* This total represents the number of persons assisted during the biennium, and not the number of placements made. Some persons have been placed several times in the process of finding the most suitable employment for the individual.

** This figure indicates average weekly earnings at the time of placement and does not show increments.

PRE-CONDITIONING CENTER

Pursuant to the law passed by the Legislature in 1945 a training center for the adult blind was opened in Greenville, N. C. on November 1, 1945. This Enterprise was made possible by the cooperative efforts of the State, Lions Clubs, local school authorities and individuals.

The Pre-Conditioning Center has been opened for the purpose of granting the adult blind the basic right to which each citizen of the State is entitled; namely, training which will meet the needs of the individual and will enable him to take his place in the community according to his abilities.

The training courses are divided into two categories: (1) Orientation or Pre-Conditioning and (2) Vocational. Students according to their needs may be admitted to pre-conditioning or vocational training or both. The maximum period for pre-conditioning training is 10 months and vocational training is 12 months.

Gardening is one of the Vocational courses taught at the Pre-Conditioning Center.

During his orientation experience his potentialities and interests will be discovered and the student will then be given training for the vocation in which he demonstrates the most interest and aptitudes. His period of vocational training will be determined by his own abilities, but will not exceed 12 months. Part of this training may take place in an actual working situation where he will be under close supervision. Arrangements for this outside work training will be made by the Rehabilitation Counselor and the supervision will be given by them and the man in charge of the business or industry in which the student is placed.

While vocational employability is the chief objective of the Pre-Conditioning Center, and the majority of the activities are directed toward this goal it is recognized that there are many factors which affect either directly or indirectly the success of the individual student. A physical restoration program designed to correct physical defects which might affect his employability is planned. Aptitude, Vocational, Intelligence, and Personality tests are given soon after the student is enrolled. These tests are given by a qualified Psychologist and the results are used as an indication of the students strengths and difficulties. If indicated psychiatric treatment is given by a trained Psychiatrist. Guidance and Counseling by trained and experienced Counselors and directed toward assisting the trainee to develop his capabilities and adjust to his handicap.

Training in wood working (left) and small animal husbandry (right) are given to those students interested in entering these vocations.

Important in the operation of the Center and the development of the students is the student government organization in which

Recreational activities are im-   Braille and. typing are required
portant in the operation of the   subjects for all students.
center.

the student body elects its own officers, and conducts affairs normally under the jurisdiction of such a body.

It is very difficult to give a clear explanation of the orientation (pre-conditioning) training as it is scheduled. This is due to the fact that much of this training takes place in a class room situation, which classes might also be vocational training in content, and in his day-to-day living at the Center and in the community of Greenville.

In learning to travel around his room, from his room to the dining room, class room, office, etc. he is learning to use Travel Aids; he is gaining experience in traveling around unfamiliar grounds; his memory is being developed, and at the same time he is acquiring a sense of obstacle awareness and auditory acuteness. It is recognized that the success with which he learns to travel is largely dependent on the amount of self-confidence which the trainee develops, and as a result he is given the minimum of assistance and the maximum of self-responsibility.

As soon as the student has learned to successfully travel around the Center he is assisted to become independent in meeting his own needs outside the Center by learning to travel around Greenville. He does his own shopping, goes to the barber shop, picture shows, etc.

The loan of railway cars on a side track and buses not in use is made to enable exploration, before use, of public facilities for travel. The student is then encouraged to take week-end trips to his home.

At the same time the trainee is learning to get around without assistance he is also learning to take care of his room, he is learning personal toiletry, proper eating habits, and the more acceptable social conventions which he will be expected to observe in his daily contacts on the outside with sighted people.

In the initial stages of his training each student is required to study the following courses:

Courses in developing memory and the remaining senses.

Elementary handicrafts.

Use of hand tools.

Simple bench assembly.

Gardening.

Braille.

Typing.

Signature writing.

Elementary English.

Arithmetic.

All students are required to take an elementary course in crafts. Chair caning is one of the subjects taught.

As orientation courses they are required for 3 reasons: (1) they develop memory, manual dexterity and the remaining senses; (2) they offer a basis for assisting the students and the counselors in determining his greatest vocational possibilities; (3) They assist him in becoming a normal citizen and taking his place in the community. It is from these introductions to the various fields of employment that he specializes in the one in which he is most likely to succeed.

Pre-Conditioning, sufficient to make the student adequate for admission to Vocational training, is reached at the point where he has made sufficient adjustments to his handicaps and to his personal situation to be able to mobilize himself vocationally. The fact that he has reached this point is determined by observation of his reactions to situations in day-to-day living; and a working knowledge of the basic skills of the blind as described above.

Since its opening, 85 students from 35 counties in the State have received training at the Center. These students were those who had been accepted as rehabilitation clients and whose maintenance and tuition were paid, in the main, from funds available through that Division.

The Lions Clubs of the State contributed $15,000.00 for permanent equipment and the State appropriation of $15,000.00 was used for additional equipment, initial supplies and materials and other expenses incidental to opening the facilities.

BUSINESS ENTERPRISES

Pursuant to the law which places upon the Commission the responsibility for maintaining employment opportunities for blind individuals who are able to work but unable to find placement in outside employment, the Commission established, by resolution, an auxiliary division known as the Bureau of Employment for the Blind.

The advisory body of this Bureau is made up of business men who have had experience in the field of merchandising and who advise the Commission on policies, rules, regulations and practices which should be established and observed in the operation of a successful business enterprise program.

Employees in the Business Enterprises program are blind or partially sighted individuals who have gone through the rehabilitation process and who have decided to make the operation of a small business their vocations. The training they receive involves the field of merchandising, salesmanship and personal responsibilities.

Daily records are kept on each unit and the employees are given an efficiency rating at the end of each six months period. Salary adjustments are made on the basis of these ratings.

The operation of a telephone exchange in a small community gives employment to this blind man who suffers with a double handicap.

The expansion of this program has been one of the main goals of the Commission during this biennium and its growth is shown in Tables I and II on pages 33 and 35.

The passage of the Randolph-Shephard Act permitted the establishment of concession stands in Federal Buildings. The one above is located in a post office.

The lobby of an office building offers an excellent location for a vending stand as the one shown above.

A stand in an industrial plant is a good location both from the standpoint of the operator and the plant employees.

WORKSHOPS

The five Workshops for the Blind established by the Commission for the Blind in cooperation with the Lions Clubs and County Associations, provide employment for ninety-five blind persons at an average weekly wage of $16.86.

The Commission furnishes all equipment, assists in payment of salaries of the Workshop Foremen, approves employment of personnel and owns the land and buildings in which two of the Shops are operating. The local Lions Clubs or County Associations assist in the management of the shops and provide many services for the blind, such as; recreation, entertainment and assistance with their housing problems. Many of the blind who have not had work experiences are trained in the shops and helped to adjust to different environments.

Due to the cancellation of all Federal Orders at the close of the war, there occurred a drop in sales and employment in the five workshops. All blind persons affected by this change have been placed in other employment.

A Social Security Plan has been inaugurated for the workshop employees, providing Hospitalization, Unemployment Compensation and Vacations with pay.

Mattress making in Asheville Work Shop.

Sewing in the Charlotte Work Shop

The Asheville Workshop for the Blind, sponsored by the Buncombe County Association for the Blind, is housed in a fireproof brick building which has been deeded to the State Commission for

Carding handkerchiefs in the Winston-Salem Work Shop

Producing cotton felt for mattresses in the
Durham Work Shop

the Blind. Mattress making and renovating is the chief post-war industry. Other activities will be added as soon as possible.

The Mecklenburg County Workshop for the Blind is operated by the Charlotte Lions Club. Sheets, pillow cases, napkins, mops and other small articles are made. Employment is given to sixteen blind persons.

Broom manufacturing in the
Greensboro Work Shop

The Industries for the Blind in Winston-Salem operate in a two-story brick building which was purchased by the Winston-Salem Lions Club. Mattresses are made, the folding, bagging and carding of handkerchiefs, carding combs, and assembling tire patching materials furnish employment to many blind workers.

The Durham Lions Club Workshop for the Blind gives employment to fourteen blind workers in the manufacture of mattresses. A new building is planned and new projects will be added as soon as space is available.

The Guilford County Workshop for the Blind is operated under the Guilford County Association for the Blind. The major industries are broom-making, mops, rubber mats, and chair repairing. A new building is needed and will be erected as soon as building material is available.

An expansion program is planned for all workshops whereby the manufacture of the useful commodities will be carried on, on an equal basis with other manufacturers. There are many projects which a blind person can do in a manufacturing plant with minimum supervision.

HOME INDUSTRIES

For sometime a Home Industry program has been in operation in sixteen counties giving steady employment to twenty-

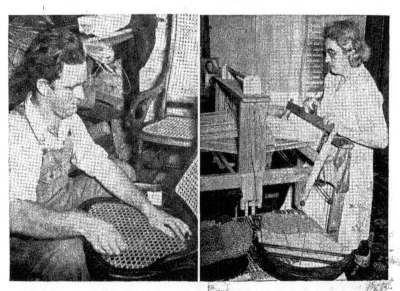

Weaving (right) and chair caning (left) are two popular home industry activities.

This housewife adds to the income of her family by making quilts for sale and by canning surplus fruits and vegetables.

seven blind persons who, for different reasons cannot leave home for employment. These individuals earn from $15.00 to $25.00 per month by preparing materials for rug manufacturers, weaving, gardening and poultry raising. While this income adds greatly to their material comforts, the earnings are not as great as the peace of mind which has been established through occupation.

Through the services of the Special Case Worker for the Blind, one-hundred and seventy-two persons in thirty-one counties are busy sewing, looping clips, assembling leather articles, chair caning, weaving and gardening. While these activities are considered to be for adjustment purposes the individuals thus engaged do supplement their incomes by the sale of the articles produced and their earnings range from $5.00 to $15.00 per month. Through this application of occupational therapy, individuals develop skills and interests which enable them to participate in the Home Industry program.

This program is sponsored by the local Lions Clubs, County Associations and interested individuals, who supply the funds for materials, supplies and equipment.

ASSISTANCE AND COOPERATION FROM OTHER
AGENCIES, GROUPS AND INDIVIDUALS

In the preceding parts of this report there has been shown the assistance and cooperation received by the North Carolina State Commission for the Blind from the Federal Security Agency, the County Commissioners and County Welfare Departments, the Lions Clubs, and the State Association for the Blind. It should again be emphasized that the blind people of North Carolina have reaped the benefits of this aid and that because of it the Commission has been able to markedly expand its services.

There are other groups and individuals who have greatly contributed to the activities of work for the blind. The majority of these have already been mentioned elsewhere but because of the quality of the contribution recognization is again given:

Ophthalmologists

North Carolina is most fortunate in having located in the various sections of the State Eye Physicians who are giving unsparingly of their time and interest to prevent blindness and wherever possible to conserve and restore vision. These Ophthalmologists give to the needy cases recommended to their care the same highly skilled, professional services received by the private patient, and without the very fine cooperation and unselfishness of these Physicians it would be impossible to have a program of prevention in North Carolina.

The Commission is also indebted to the many private physicians who give treatment to persons referred for general medical attention by the Ophthalmologists. The eye difficulties of these patients are the result of disease or abnormal conditions in other parts of the body, for the eye is often called "a thermometer to bodily conditions." Many indigent persons with defective vision coming under the care of the Commission have diseases of the blood vessels, kidneys, brain or other parts of the body which are first discovered by the Eye Physician. Diseased tonsils and other bodily infections in children are so often the cause of impaired vision, which condition if not detected by an Eye Physician and corrected may impair the efficiency not only of the eye but of other vital organs of the body.

Other Agencies and Individuals

The State Federation of Women's Clubs have taken work for the blind as one of their major projects. Individual clubwomen are rendering personal services to the blind as a part of their general program.

The State Welfare Department, the State Department of Education, the State Board of Health, the County School and Health Officials, the local private Welfare Agencies and Hospitals have given valuable assistance in the development of its work.

The State School for the Blind has given fine cooperation to the Commission in the development of its work.

Rotary, Kiwanis, American Business Men's Club, the Variety Club, Exchange Clubs, P. T. A.'s and other organizations have cooperated in their local communities.

The following organizations outside of the State aid the Commission in the development of its work: The American Foundation for the Blind, National Industries for the Blind, The National Society for the Prevention of Blindness, The National Society for the Blind, The Seeing Eye, The Washington Society for the Blind and The National Rehabilitation Association.

RECOMMENDATIONS

The preceding report of the work of the Commission has presented a brief review of the services rendered to the blind and needy visually handicapped of North Carolina during the past biennium. This report also calls attention to some of the unmet needs.

The members of the Commission appreciate the difficult problems of state financing and realize that each session of the Legislature is faced with the necessity of trying to keep the state budget at as low a figure as possible. While the budget request of the Commission does represent an increase over the funds appropriated in prior years it does not provide for meeting all of the urgent needs of the visually handicapped in North Carolina. The Commission is confining its request for increased funds to the following six needs:

First, $45,000 additional funds are requested to provide matching funds for the expanded rehabilitation services available to North Carolina under Federal legislation. These funds are necessary to provide training, medical examinations, corrective surgery, transportation, hospitalization, placement equipment and prosthetic devices needed in the rehabilitation of blind individuals who, after rehabilitation services are given, are removed from direct relief rolls and become self supporting.

Second, $153,922 additional funds are requested for direct relief grants for the needy blind. According to the laws of North Carolina all persons eligible for Aid to the Blind grants are the responsibility of the North Carolina State Commission for the Blind. At the present, there are approximately 2600 individuals receiving aid and 1000 eligible persons to whom the Commission cannot make grants because of insufficient funds. The money requested will permit the Commission to make average monthly grants of $25.00 for the first year of the biennium and $27.00 for the second year of the biennium.

Third, $50,000 is requested for the maintenance and operation of the Pre-conditioning Center. This Center is a training facility for the adult blind and while part of the funds necessary for its maintenance and operation are available through tuition and maintenance fees from rehabilitation clients the money available from this source is not sufficient to provide training opportunities to all of the blind persons who are in need of this service. It is planned to use the Center to provide personal adjustment and home industry training opportunities to blind individuals who are not eligible for other types of rehabilitation services.

Fourth, $50,000 is requested for County Administrative purposes. At the present the counties are providing part of the salary and travel of the Special Case Workers for the Blind and the Federal Government the remainder. At the present these salaries are inadequate and the amount of travel funds alloted each Case Worker is not sufficient to permit proper covering of the territories involved. The majority of the Case Workers cover an area of from 2 to 6 counties, and while the counties are responsible for part of the costs of guide service and car expenses within the county no funds are available to the worker for inter-county travel. The Commission believes that in order to maintain the staff of Special Case Workers the state should participate in the payment of their salaries and travel.

In addition to the salary and travel of the Special Case Worker for the Blind part of the fund that is being requested will be used for necessary clerical staff. At the present there is no clerical assistance available to Special Case Workers for the Blind and other staff members who work on an area basis. Such assistance is essential if the professional staff is to be released from the necessity of spending a large part of its time in performing clerical functions.

Fifth, $45,406 is requested for additional administrative expenses of the Commission.

$2,220 of this amount is to increase the salary of the Executive Secretary to $6,000 per year. The Commission believes that the size of the Agency and the responsibility of the Executive Secretary have expanded to the point where this increase is justified.

$7,320 is requested to employ an Administrative Assistant. This is a new position which is necessary due to the growth of the Agency and the amount of administrative work which must be accomplished.

$18,680 is requested to pay the part (one third) of the Field Representatives and Medical Social Workers salaries that is now being paid from Federal funds. The Federal Vocational Rehabilitation authorities have taken the position that the payment of the salaries of these persons is a state responsibility.

$10,680 additional funds are requested to pay the part (one third) of the travel of the persons mentioned above which is now being paid from these Federal funds. The Commission has been advised that this will not be permissable after July 1, 1947 since it is interpreted to be a state responsibility.

$4,320 is requested to provide a $120.00 yearly increment for the salary of the Workshop Foremen, the Manager of Business Enterprises and the administrative clerical staff.

$2,186 in addition to that already appropriated is requested for administrative costs such as postage, printing, repairs and alterations, supplies and materials, office equipment and general expenses. This additional amount is needed to meet the demands of an expanded program.

Sixth, $53,526 additional funds are requested for an over-all increment of 15% in the salaries of the staff. This increase is based on the present compensation schedule. The Commission believes that the increase in the cost of living makes it mandatory to revise the present salary ranges in order to permit the retention and recruitment of an adequate staff. Because of the higher salaries offered many efficient employees have resigned from the Agency to accept employment in private industry or Federal Government Agencies and it has become increasingly difficult to recruit qualified persons to fill the vacancies.

Permanent Improvements

Pursuant to an act of the Legislature of 1945 the North Carolina State Commission for the Blind opened a Pre-Conditioning Center for the purposes of training and rehabilitating visually handicapped persons. No provisions were made however for adequately housing such activities. The temporary quarters which are now being used are an abandoned N.Y.A. residence center which are loaned to the Commission by the public schools of Greenville, North Carolina. There are nine small separate dilapidated units of very temporary structure and when the Commission accepted it for use it was with the understanding that only the necessary repairs would be made to make it usable until a permanant facility could be obtained. Prior to their being taken over by the Commission the buildings were occupied by a troop of Marines who left them in very poor condition and the expenses involved in putting them into repair to be used for more than a temporary period would be totally impracticable, since it would require major alterations including the installation of at least six furnaces or a central heating plant. In addition, the school Board of Greenville is planning to use the land on which to build a public school, and the Commission has agreed to vacate the premises as soon as their building program can begin.

The lot on which to construct a building in Raleigh is available at no additional expense to the State and by locating it in the Capital City it would afford office space for the Administrative staff of the Commission which would relieve the over-crowded condition of the present offices. In addition it is most desirable to have this training center close to the Administrative staff in order that close supervision can be given without the expense of excessive travel. By locating the Center in Raleigh it would also be near the central part of the State and would, therefore, be more accessible to the persons whom it is intended to serve.

The year's experience since the Center was opened has definitely proven that the far-sighted vision of the Legislature of 1945 was based on the sound judgment that the adult blind of North Carolina needed and would take advantage of training opportunities if offered them. The request for $275,000 for the construction of a permanent building in which to house these activities is therefore considered by the Commission to be justified.

APPENDIX I

Data by counties giving the age, diagnosis, and vision before and after treatment of the 1,163 persons removed from the classification of blindness.

INFORMATIONAL DATA ON 1,163 PERSONS REMOVED FROM CLASSIFICATION OF BLINDNESS
JULY 1, 1944—JUNE 30, 1946

NOTE: 20/20 is normal vision, that is, the individual can see an object at 20 feet which he is supposed to see at that distance. 20/200 means that the person must be within 20 feet of an object to see it while he should be able to see it 200 feet away. The numerator in this fraction is always the distance at which the person should be able to see if vision were normal.

In the table below, "L.P." means "Light Perception"; "H.M." "Hand Movements"; "F.C." "Finger Count"; "Nil" means "Total Blindness."

County	Age	Diagnosis	Vision Before Medical Care Given		Vision After Medical Care Given	
			Right Eye	Left Eye	Right Eye	Left Eye
Alamance	67	Cataract-Chorio-Retinitis	20/400	Nil	20/50	Nil
Alexander	11	Hyperopia-Astigmatism	20/100	20/100	20/30	20/30
"	9	Hyperopia	20/100	20/200	20/20	20/20
"	10	Hyperopia	20/200	20/200	20/20	20/20
"	13	Myopia	20/200	20/200	20/30	20/30
Alleghany	7	Congenital Nystagmus-Myopia	F.C. 8 ft.	F.C. 10 ft.	20/50	20/70
"	65	Hyperopia	Nil	20/200	Nil	20/30
Anson	16	Hyperopia	20/200	20/200	20/70	20/70
"	12	Hyperopia-Astigmatism	20/200	20/200	20/20	20/40
"	77	Surgical Aphakia	F. C.	F. C.	20/70	20/50
Ashe	86	Ametropia-Presbyopia	20/200	20/200	20/30	20/30
"	74	Cataracts-Surgical Aphakia	10/200	8/200	20/70	20/70
"	59	Hyperopia-Presbyopia	20/100	20/100 .	20/20	20/30
"	13	Hyperopia	20/100	20/200	20/70	20/100
Avery	25	Myopia	20/100	20/100	20/80	20/80
"	5	Squint-Hyperopia	20/200	20/200	20/20	20/20
"	26	Myopia-Astigmatism	20/200	20/200	20/40	20/25
"	65	Hyperopia-Astigmatism	20/100	20/100	20/20	20/20
"	66	Cataract-Phthisis Bulbi	20/100	Nil	20/30	Nil
"	48	Keratitis	20/200	20/200	02/30	20/40
"	57	Hyperopia-Presbyopia	20/200	20/200	20/20	20/20
"	61	Hyperopia-Presbyopia	20/200	20/100	20/40	20/20
Beaufort	14	Myopia	20/200	20/200	14/20	14/20
"	9	Myopia	20/200	20/200	14/20	14/20
"	60	Glaucoma-Hyperopia	Nil	20/200	Nil	20/15
"	30	Hyperopia-Astigmatism	20/200	20/200	20/70	20/70
"	75	Cataract-Surgical Aphakia	20/200	20/200	20/40	20/40
"	11	Myopia-Astigmatism	20/100	20/100	20/80	20/80
"	71	Myopia	20/100	20/100	20/60	20/60
"	55	Hyperopia	20/200	20/200	20/20	20/20
"	65	Hyperopia Presbyopia	20/200	20/200	20/30	20/30
Bertie	28	Astigmatism	20/400	20/400	20/100	20/70
"	47	Presbyopia Hyperopia	20/100	20/100	20/20	20/20
"	80	Cataract-Surgical Aphakia	20/200	F.C. 5ft.	20/40	F.C. 5 ft.
"	51	Presbyopia-Hyperopia	20/100	20/200	20/20	20/20
"	17	Myopia-Astigmatism	20/200	20/200	20/50	20/50
"	32	Progressive Myopia	20/200	10/200	20/70	20/50
"	65	Pterygium-Cataract	F. C.	20/200	F. C.	20/50
"	60	Hyperopia Presbyopia	20/100	20/100	20/50	20/20

County	Age	Diagnosis	Vision Before Medical Care Given		Vision After Medical Care Given	
			Right Eye	Left Eye	Right Eye	Left Eye
Bladen	63	Cataract-Surgical Aphakia	H.M. 2ft.	F.C. 2ft.	H.M. 2ft.	20/60
"	87	Surgical Aphakia-Cataract	20/200	Nil	20/40	Nil
"	11	Myopia-Astigmatism	20/100	20/100	20/50	20/50
Brunswick	43	Cataract-Surgical-Aphakia	F.C. 5ft.	F.C. 5ft.	20/15	20/15
"	25	Cataract Surgical Aphakia	20/100	F. C.	20/30	20/30
Buncombe	65	Presbyopia-Hyperopia	15/200	15/200	20/20	20/20
"	51	Hyperopia Presbyopia	7/200	14/200	20/50	20/50
"	64	Hyperopia-Presbyopia	20/200	20/200	20/20	20/20
"	49	Hyperopia Presbyopia	6/200	5/200	20/40	20/40
"	12	Strabismus-Hyperopia	20/200	20/100	20/200	20/30
	24	Anisometropia	20/200	10/200	20/30	20/70
"	63	Cataract-Surgical Aphakia	20/400	20/400	20/50	20/50
"	54	Hyperopia-Presbyopia	20/100	20/100	20/40	20/40
"	61	Cataract-Opacities	10/200	10/200	10/200	20/25
"	60	Hyperopia-Presbyopia	12/200	14/200	20/30	20/30
	49	Cataract-Dacrocystitis	20/200	20/200	20/50	20/50
	76	Cataract-Hyperopia-Presbyopia	L. P.	10/200	L. P.	20/70
	60	Hyperopia-Presbyopia	12/200	12/200	20/20	20/20
"	67	Hypermetropia-Presbyopia	20/100	20/200	20/20	20/20
"	15	Hyperopia	20/200	20/200	20/70	20/70
	9	Strabismus-Hyperopia-Astigmatism	20/100	20/100	20/50	20/50
"	62	Hyperopia	20/100	20/100	20/30	20/25
Burke	26	Myopia-Astigmatism	5/200	10/200	20/40	20/40
"	47	Myopia-Astigmatism	20/200	20/200	20/40	20/200
"	70	Cataract-Surgical Aphakia	20/200	20/200	20/60	20/60
"	66	Surgical Aphakia	L. P.	L. P.	20/20	20/20
"	48	Cataracts-Surgical Aphakia	L. P.	L. P.	L. P.	20/40
"	67	Astigmatism-Hyperopia-Phthisis Bulbi	20/160	Nil	20/25	Nil
"	45	Cataract-Surgical Aphakia	L. P.	L. P.	L. P.	20/40
"	72	Surgical Aphakia-Cataracts	20/100	F.C. 3ft.	20/100	20/50
"	70	Cataract-Surgical Aphakia	L. P.	F.C. 2ft.	L. P.	20/30
Cabarrus	72	Hyperopia-Astigmatism	20/100	20/100	20/30	20/30
	61	Cataract-Surgical Aphakia	F.C. 10ft.	8/200	20/30	8/200
"	9	Astigmatism	20/200	20/200	20/30	20/30
"	64	Hyperopia-Presbyopia	20/200	20/200	20/20	20/20
	64	Cataract-Surgical Aphakia	1/200	L. P.	1/200	20/24
"	30	Astigmatism	20/200	20/200	20/80	20/200
"	53	Presbyopia-Hyperopia	20/200	20/200	20/20	20/20
	66	Presbyopia-Hyperopia	20/200	20/200	20/20	20/20
	53	Hyperopia-Presbyopia	20/200	20/200	20/20	20/20
	12	Myopia	20/200	20/200	20/20	20/20
"	9	Myopia	4/200	4/200	20/30	20/30
"	12	Astigmatism	20/200	20/200	20/20	20/30
"	13	Astigmatism	20/100	20/100	20/20	20/20
"	11	Astigmatism	20/200	20/200	20/80	20/80
	11	Astigmatism-Hyperopia	20/200	20/200	20/15	20/15
	14	Myopia	20/200	20/200	20/20	20/20
	8	Hyperopia	20/100	20/200	20/30	20/30
	14	Myopia	20/200	20/200	20/20	20/20
	15	Myopia	15/200	15/200	20/20	20/20
	9	Hyperopia-Amblyopia	20/200	20/200	20/20	20/20
"	71	Cataracts-Surgical Aphakia	5/200	4/200	20/25	20/25
"	74	Hyperopia-Presbyopia	20/100	20/100	20/20	20/20
"	57	Hyperopia-Presbyopia	20/100	20/100	20/20	20/20
	73	Hyperopia-Presbyopia	12/200	15/200	20/20	20/20

County	Age	Diagnosis	Vision Before Medical Care Given		Vision After Medical Care Given	
			Right Eye	Left Eye	Right Eye	Left Eye
Cabarrus	80	Myopia-Presbyopia	25/100	25/100	20/30	20/30
"	71	Hyperopia-Amblyopia-Presbyopia	7/200	5/200	20/100	20/20
"	73	Retinitis-Hyperopia	5/200	20/200	5/200	20/40
"	61	Cataract-Surgical Aphakia	F.C. 10in.	8/200	20/33	8/200
"	70	Cataract-Surgical Aphakia	3/200	L. P.	20/30	L. P.
"	7	Hyperopia	20/100	20/100	20/30	20/30
Caldwell	54	Hyperopia-Presbyopia	20/100	20/100	20/20	20/20
"	54	Myopia	20/500	20/500	20/20	20/20
"	84	Cataract-Hyperopia-Presbyopia	Nil	20/200	Nil	20/30
"	50	Hyperopia-Presbyopia	20/100	20/100	20/20	20/20
"	26	Myopia	20/100	20/100	20/25	20/25
"	15	Myopia	20/200	20/300	20/20	20/20
"	18	Coloboma-Choroiditis-Surgical Aphakia	L. P.	F.C. 6 ft.	L. P.	20/50
"	41	Hyperopia-Retinitis	20/200	20/200	20/50	20/70
"	55	Hyperopia-Persbyopia	20/200	20/200	20/30	20/30
"	9	Nystagmus-Hypreopia	20/400	20/400	20/70	20/40
"	38	Myopia-Chorio-Retinitis	H. M.	20/400	H. M.	20/40
"	74	Hyperopia	10/400	15/400	20/80	20/40
"	22	Myopia	20/200	20/200	20/30	20/30
"	47	Coloboma-Chorio-Retinitis- Surgical Aphakia	L. P.	F.C. 3 ft.	L. P.	20/30
"	65	Hyperopia-Presbyopia	20/200	20/200	20/20	20/20
"	15	Myopia	20/200	20/200	20/25	20/25
Camden	68	Surgical Aphakia	Nil	F.C. 3ft.	Nil	20/50
Carteret	61	Optic Atrophy-Myopia	Nil	20/200	Nil	20/50
"	66	Cataract-Surgical Aphakia	20/200	20/200	20/200	20/25
Catawba	27	Myopia	20/200	20/200	20/25	20/25
"	16	Myopia	20/300	20/300	20/25	20/25
"	80	Cataracts-Surgical Aphakia	20/800	20/800	20/800	20/50
"	27	Conical Cornea-Contact Lenses	20/400	F.C. 3 ft.	20/40	20/40
"	72	Cataract-Surgical Aphakia	30/100	L. P.	20/100	20/40
"	75	Cataract-Surgical Aphakia	L. P.	5/200	20/25	20/25
Chatham	13	Myopia	15/200	20/200	20/30	20/30
"	15	Hyperopia-Astigmatism	20/100	20/100	20/20	20/20
Cherokee	66	Squint-Cataract-Surgical Aphakia	20/200	20/400	20/50	20/400
"	16	Hyperopia	20/100	20/200	20/20	20/20
"	54	Hyperopia-Presbyopia	20/100	20/100	20/20	20/20
"	46	Trauma	Nil	20/200	Nil	20/50
"	39	Strabismus-Nystagmus-Myopia	20/100	20/100	20/100	20/70
"	21	Retinitis Pigmentosa-Myopia	20/100	20/100	20/70	20/50
"	38	Glaucoma-Myopia	20/200	F.C. 1 ft.	20/25	F.C. 1ft.
"	16	Hyperopia-Astigmatism	20/200	20/200	20/30	20/30
"	19	Nystagmus-Hyperopia	20/100	20/100	20/70	20/100
"	72	Cataracts-Surgical Aphakia	20/200	20/100	20/50	20/70
"	63	Hyperopia-Astigmatism-Presbyopia	20/200	20/100	20/40	20/40
"	36	Hyperopia	20/200	20/200	20/20	20/20
"	50	Presbyopia-Hyperopia-Astigmatism	20/100	20/100	20/20	20/20
"	66	Hyperopia-Astigmatism	20/200	20/200	20/20	20/20
"	65	Hyperopia-Astigmatism-Presbyopia	20/100	20/100	20/30	20/30
"	43	Astigmatism-Hyperopia	20/100	20/200	20/20	20/30
"	20	Hyperopia	20/100	20/100	20/70	20/50
"	40	Strabismus-Nystagmus-Hyperopia	20/100	20/100	20/100	20/70
"	13	Myopia	20/100	20/100	20/20	20/20
"	13	Myopia	20/100	20/100	20/40	20/40
"	7	Hyperopia-Astigmatism	20/200	20/200	20/70	20/50

County	Age	Diagnosis	Vision Before Medical Care Given		Vision After Medical Care Given	
			Right Eye	Left Eye	Right Eye	Left Eye
Cherokee	20	Myopia-Astigmatism	20/200	20/200	20/20	20/20
"	10	Astigmatism	20/100	20/200	20/100	20/40
"	67	Hyperopia-Astigmatism-Presbyopia	5/200	20/200	20/20	20/20
::	15	Myopia-Astigmatism	10/200	10/200	20/20	20/20
"	80	Blepharitis-Cataracts-Surgical Aphakia	F.C. 5ft.	F.C. 5ft.	20/70	20/30
Chowan	12	Hyperopia-Astigmatism	20/100	20/100	20/30	20/30
"	66	Cataract-Pterygium-Surgical Aphakia	20/100	Nil	20/70	Nil
Clay	14	Hyperopia	20/100	20/100	20/20	20/30
"	48	Hyperopia	20/200	20/100	20/30	20/30
"	13	Myopia-Astigmatism	20/100	20/200	20/30	20/30
Cleveland	37	Filtering Cicartix-Hyperopia	Nil	10/200	Nil	20/40
"	9	Astigmatism	20/100	20/100	20/20	20/20
"	72	Cataract-Surgical Aphakia	F.C. 1ft.	L. P.	20/40	C.F. 6ft.
..	58	Cataract-Surgical Aphakie	F.C. 5ft.	L. P.	20/40	F.C. 5ft.
	11	Hyperopia	20/100	20/100	20/30	20/30
	80	Cataract-Surgical Aphakia	20/100	20/100	20/70	20/100
	9	Hyperopia-Astigmatism	20/200	20/100	20/30	20/30
	66	Hyperopia-Presbyopia	15/200	15/200	20/50	20/20
	11	Myopia-Astigmatism	20/400	20/300	20/30	20/30
.-'	13	Myopia	20/100	20/100	20/30	20/30
"	63	Coloboma-Iris Atrophy-Hyperopia	10/200	Nil	20/50	Nil
Columbus	67	Myopia	20/200	20/200	20/20	20/20
"	72	Cataract-Surgical Aphakia	20/200	Nil	20/70	Nil
"	73	Cataract-Presbyopia	20/200	20/200	20/40	20/40
..	71	Cataract	Nil	20/100	Nil	20/30
	73	Hyperopia-Astigmatism	20/100	20/100	20/30	20/30
..	80	Cataract-Presbyopia	20/100	20/100	20/40	20/40
	76	Optic Atrophy-Myopia-Astigmatism	F. C..3ft.	20/100	F.C. 3ft.	20/30
"	11	Edema of Retina	20/200	20/300	20/30	20/200
"	66	Myopia	20/400	20/400	20/30	20/30
"	76	Cataract-Surgical Aphakia	L. P.	20/400	L. P.	20/70
Craven	67	Optic Atrophy-Hyperopia	20/100	Nil	20/50	Nil
"	70	Hyperopia-Presbyopia	20/100	20/100	20/50	20/50
"	65	Hyperopia-Presbyopia	20/100	20/100	20/20	20/20
"	11	Myopia-Astigmatism	20/100	20/100	20/15	20/20
'	7	Hyperopia	20/100	20/100	20/100	20/70
"	10	Astigmatism	20/100	20/100	20/30	20/30
"	65	Cataract-Surgical Aphakia	20/300	L. P.	20/30	20/30
Cumberland	66	Hyperopia-Cataract-Surgical Aphakia	20/200	20/200	20/40	20/40
"	12	Nystagmus Hyperopia	20/200	20/200	20/40	20/100
"	10	Astigmatism-Amblyopia	L. P.	20/200	20/200	20/30
"	65	Astigmatism-Strabismus	20/200	20/200	20/40	20/100
"	12	Astigmatism	20/100	20/100	20/40	20/40
"	10	Astigmatism	20/100	20/100	20/20	20/20
	11	Hyperopia-Astigmatism	20/200	20/100	20/20	20/30
"	44	Astigmatism	20/200	20/200	20/30	20/30
	54	Hyperopia-Presbyopia	20/200	20/200	20/20	20/20
	61	Hyperopia-Presbyopia	Nil	20/100	Nil	20/20
::	17	Myopia-Astigmatism	20/200	20/200	2/020	20/20
	11	Hyperopia-Astigmatism	20/100	20/100	20/40	20/40
..	27	Hyperopia	20/100	20/100	20/50	20/50
	11	Hyperopia	20/100	20/100	20/30	20/30

County	Age	Diagnosis	Vision Before Medical Care Given		Vision After Medical Care Given	
			Right Eye	Left Eye	Right Eye	Left Eye
Cumberland	8	Hyperopia	20/100	20/100	20/20	20/20
"	12	Astigmatism-Amblyopia	20/200	20/200	20/200	20/40
"	47	Hyperopia-Astigmatism	20/100	20/100	20/20	20/20
	48	Hyperopia-Presbyopia	20/100	20/100	20/20	20/20
"	11	Hyperopia	20/100	20/100	20/20	20/20
	12	Astigmatism	20/100	20/100	20/30	20/30
"	51	Astigmatism-Presbyopia	20/100	20/100	20/20	20/20
	62	Astigmatism-Presbyopia	20/200	20/200	20/20	20/20
"	13	Astigmatism-Myopia	20/400	20/200	20/100	20/40
	9	Hyperopia-Astigmatism	20/400	20/400	20/40	20/40
	11	Hyperopia-Astigmatism	20/20	20/200	20/20	20/20
	12	Astigmatism	20/100	20/100	20/20	20/20
	11	Hyperopia	20/200	20/200	20/20	20/25
	76	Cataract-Surgical Aphakia	20/100	20/100	20/40	20/40
	6	Strabismus-Hyperopia	Nil	20/100	Nil	20/50
"	23	Intraocular Infection-Hyperopia	20/200	20/200	20/40	20/40
	8	Astigmatism	20/100	20/100	20/20	20/20
	10	Astigmatism	20/100	20/100	20/20	20/20
	11	Astigmatism	20/200	20/200	20/20	20/20
	47	Optic Atrophy-Astigmatism	Nil	20/100	Nil	20/20
	52	Extropia-Amblyopia Hyperopia	L. P.	L. P.	20/50	20/200
	14	Hyperopia-Astigmatism	20/100	20/400	20/30	20/30
	70	Cataract-Arterio-Sclerosis-Surgical Aphakia	Nil	20/200	Nil	20/50
	69	Surgical Aphakia	F. C.	F. C.	20/30	20/20
	67	Cataracts-Surgical Aphakia	F. C.	F. C.	20/30	20/30
	75	Arterio-sclerosis-Hyperopia	20/100	20/100	20/40	20/40
	60	Presbyopia-Astigmatism	20/200	20/200	20/20	20/20
	16	Astigmatism	20/200	20/200	20/20	20/20
	69	Surgical Aphakia	C. F.	C. F.	20/20	20/30
"	68	Surgical Aphakia	C. F.	C. F.	C.F.	20/40
	75	Cataract-Surgical Aphakia	20/200	20/200	20/20	20/20
	73	Cataract-Surgical Aphakia	C. F.	C. F.	20/80	20/80
	72	Cataract-Surgical Aphakia	20/100	20/100	20/40	20/40
	8	Hyperopia	20/100	20/100	20/20	20/40
	12	Hyperopia	20/200	20/200	20/40	20/40
	21	Hyperopia	20/100	20/100	20/40	20/46
"	67	Hyperopia-Presbyopia	20/100	20/100	20/20	20/20
	65	Hyperopia-Presbyopia	20/100	20/100	20/20	20/20
	45	Hyperopia	20/100	20/100	20/20	20/20
	12	Hyperopia	20/200	20/200	20/20	20/20
	10	Astigmatism	20/100	20/100	20/30	20/30
	11	Astigmatism	20/200	20/200	20/30	20/30
	46	Cataracts-Surgical Aphakia	20/200	20/200	20/70	20/200
	16	Hyperopia	20/400	20/300	20/20	20/20
	47	Hyperopia	20/100	20/100	20/20	20/20
	13	Hyperopia	20/100	20/200	20/20	20/20
"	44	Cataract-Surgical Aphakia	20/200	L. P.	20/50	L. P.
	62	Hyperopia-Presbyopia	Nil	20/100	Nil	20/20
	51	Hyperopia-Presbyopia	20/100	20/100	20/20	20/20
	10	Hyperopia-Astigmatism	20/100	L. P.	20/30	L. P.
	65	Cataract-Surgical Aphakia	20/200	20/200	20/50	20/50
	58	Presbyopia-Hyperopia	20/200	20/200	20/30	20/30

County	Age	Diagnosis	Vision Before Medical Care Given		Vision After Medical Care Given	
			Right Eye	Left Eye	Right Eye	Left Eye
Cumberland	64	Presbyopia	20/100	20/100	20/30	20/30
"	70	Cataract-Surgical Aphakia	L. P.	L. P.	20/60	20/60
"	65	Astigmatism-Myopia	20/200	20/200	20/20	20/20
	52	Astigmatism-Myopia	20/100	20/100	20/40	20/40
	15	Astigmatism-Myopia	20/100	20/100	20/20	20/20
"	13	Astigmatism-Myopia	20/100	20/100	20/20	20/20
	13	Hyperopia	20/100	20/100	20/20	20/20
	7	Astigmatism-Hyperopia	20/100	20/100	20/50	20/50
	74	Hyperopia-Presbyopia	20/100	20/100	20/20	20/20
	74	Hyperopia	20/100	20/100	20/20	20/20
	63	Hyperopia-Presbyopia	20/200	20/200	20/200	20/40
	33	Hyperopia	20/100	20/100	20/20	20/20
	75	Astigmatism	20/400	20/400	20/400	20/70
	9	Astigmatism	20/200	20/200	20/20	20/20
	6	Astigmatism	20/100	20/100	20/20	20/20
	14	Astigmatism	20/100	20/100	20/50	20/50
	67	Astigmatism	20/100	20/100	20/40	20/30
	70	Cataract-Surgical Aphakia	20/100	20/100	20/40	20/100
	70	Cataract-Surgical Aphakia	L. P.	L. P.	L. P.	20/60
	69	Surgical Aphakia	20/400	Nil	20/30	Nil
	66	Cataract-Surgical Aphakia	20/200	20/200	20/20	20/20
"	60	Cataract-Surgical Aphakia	20/200	L P	20/50	L. P.
Currituck	46	Myopia	20/200	20/200	20/40	20/40
"	69	Myopia-Presbyopia	5/200	L. P.	20/50	L. P.
"	79	Hyperopia-Presbyopia	20/200	20/200	20/40	20/40
"	65	Hyperopia-Presbyopia	10/200	20/200	20/40	20/30
Currituck	73	Senile Cataract-Surgical Aphakia	20/200	20/200	20/50	20/50
"	60	Opacity of Lens-Surgical Aphakia	F. C.	20/200	F. C.	20/50
"	15	Hyperopia-Astigmatism	20/200	20/200	20/70	20/70
	62	Bilateral Cataract-Surgical Aphakia	1. P.	F C.	L. P.	20/50
	69	Myopia	F.C. 18in.	F.C 18 in	20/100	20/70
"	49	Hyperopia	20/100	20/100	20/30	20/30
Dare	46	Hyperopia	6/200	6/200	20/60	20/60
"	80	Myopia-Astigmatism	10/200	10/200	20/30	20/50
"	73	Surgical Aphakia	20/200	10/200	20/200	20/50
"	63	Hyperopia-Presbyopia	10/200	10/200	20/50	20/50
"	62	Cataract-Surgical Aphakia	20/100	20/200	20/30	20/60
"	62	Hyperopia	20/100	20/100	20/70	20/100
"	52	Hyperopia	20/100	20/200	20/20	20/30
Davidson	81	Cataract-Surgical Aphakia	F. C.	F. C.	18/200	20/40
"	69	Cataract-Surgical Aphakia	20/400	F. C.	F.C. 2 ft.	20/30
"	43	Hyperopia-Presbyopia	20/100	20/100	20/20	20/20
"	44	Surgical Aphakia	20/200	20/200	20/200	20/20
"	8	Hyperopia-Astigmatism	20/180	20/180	20/35	20/35
Davie	14	Ametropia	20/200	20/200	20/20	20/20
"	12	Ametropia	20/200	20/200	20/20	20/20
"	38	Ametropia	20/100	20/100	20/20	20/30
"	26	Myopia	6/200	6/200	20/40	20/40
"	74	Hyperopia	20/100	20/100	20/70	20/30
Duplin	73	Myopia	6/200	6/400	20/60	20/400
"	67	Presbyopia-Myopia	20/100	20/200	20/60	20/70
"	11	Hyperopia	20/100	20/100	20/25	20/25
"	44	Myopia	10/200	10/200	20/30	20/30

County	Age	Diagnosis	Vision Before Medical Care Given		Vision After Medical Care Given	
			Right Eye	Left Eye	Right Eye	Left Eye
Duplin	66	Cataract-Surgical Aphakia	L. P.	F.C. 5ft.	L. P.	20/40
"	73	Cataract-Chorio-retinris-Surgical Aphakia	20/200	H.M.	20/20	H. M.
"	63	Pterygium-Ectropion-Cataract-Surgical Cor.	L. P.	F. C.1ft.	20/100	20/50.
"	14	Myopia	20/400	20/400	20/50	20/50.
"	10	Myopia	20/300	20/300	20/40	20/40.
"	14	Hyperopia-Amblyopia	20/200	20/200	20/200	20/30
"	66	Myopia-Presbyopia	10/200	10/200	20/50	20/50.
"	17	Cataracts-Surgical Aphakia	L. P.	L. P.	L. P.	20/20
"	87	Extropia-Optic Atrophy-Hyperopia	L. P.	20/400	L. P.	20/50 .
Durham	68	Cataract-Surgical Aphakia	F.C. 2 ft.	5/200	20/40	5/200
"	68	Hyperopia	20/200	20/200	20/20	20/20
"	14	Hyperopia	20/200	20/200	20/20	20/20
	65	Hyperopia-Presbyopia	20/400	20/400	20/25	20/25 .
	8	Myopia	20/100	20/100	20/25	20/25
	90	Myopia	20/400	20/100	20/80	20/40
"	70	Cataract-Surgical Aphakia	F.C. 2 ft.	20/200	20/50	20/60
	60	Cataract-Surgical Aphakia	20/200	L. P.	20/200	20/70
	53	Cataract-Surgical Aphakia.	L. P.	F. C.	L. P.	20/60
	70	Surgical Aphakia	F.C. 4 ft.	F.C. 4ft.	20/25	F.C. 2 ft.
	72	Hyperopia-Presbyopia	F.C. 7 ft.	10/100	20/50	20/25
	51	Corneal Scar-Hyperopia	H. M.	20/400	H. M.	20/50.
	10	Myopia-Astigmatism	20/200	20/200	20/40	20/40.
"	29	Cataracts-Glaucoma-Surgical Aphakia	20/400	F. C.	20/50	20/400
	56	Presbyopia-Hyperopia	20/200	5/400	20/20	20/400
	75	Cataracts-Surgical Aphakia	20/200	20/200	20/40	20/50
"	7	Myopia	20/100	20/100	20/20	20/20
"	12	Myopia-Astigmatism	20/200	20/100	20/20	20/20
"	14	Astigmatism	20/100	20/100	20/20	20/20.
"	19	Myopia	20/400	5/200	20/70	20/80
"	10	Myopia	20/200	20/200	20/30	20/30
"	13	Myopia	20/100	20/200	20/20	20/20
"	10	Myopia	20/200	20/200	20/20	20/20
	11	Myopia-Astigmatism	10/400	10/400	20/20	20/20
	75	Cataract-Surgical Aphakia	20/100	20/100	20/50	20/50
	52	Hyperopia-Presbyopia	20/200	20/200	20/20	20/20
	43	Hyperopia	20/200	20/200	20/20	20/20
	71	Cataracts-Surgical Aphakia	F.C. 5 ft.	F.C. 2ft.	F.C. 5ft.	20/25
"	75	Presbyopia-Hyperopia-Hypertension	20/200	20/400	20/40	20/25
	22	Myopia	20/400	20/200	20/20	20/20
	21	Myopia-Nystagmus	F.C. 2 ft.	20/400	20/100	20/50 ..
	9	Myopia-Astigmatism-Squint	20/100	20/100	22/400	20/40
	25	Scarred Cornea-Hyperopia	15/400	15/400	20/20	20/20 .
	67	Thrombosis-Cataract-Surgical Aphakia	L. P.	F. C.	L. P.	20/80
	71	Cataracts-Surgical Aphakia	F.C. 5 ft.	F.C. 2ft.	F.C. 5ft.	20/25
	12	Hyperopia-Astigmatism	20/100	20/200	20/50	20/60 .
	75	Hyperopia	20/200	20/200	20/25	20/30
	64	Presbyopia-Hyperopia	20/100	20/100	20/20	20/40
	76	Cataracts-Surgical Aphakia	10/400	20/200	20/30	20/200
"	77	Lenticular Debris-Cataracts-Surgical Aphakia	10/400	10/400	20/70	20/70 .

County	Age	Diagnosis	Vision Before Medical Care Given		Vision After Medical Care Given	
			Right Eye	Left Eye	Right Eye	Left Eye
Durham	45	Ret. Atrophy-Macular Deg. Hyperopia	20/100	Nil	20/40	Nil
"	55	Cataracts-Surgical Aphakia	20/400	L. P.	20/50	L. P.
"	58	Cataracts-Surgical Aphakia	L. P.	F. C.	L. P.	20/50
"	8	Myopia	20/100	20/100	20/20	20/20
"	60	Hyperopia-Astigmatism-Presbyopia	20/200	20/200	20/20	20/20
"	72	Myopia-Presbyopia	20/300	20/300	20/20	20/20
"	12	Astigmatism	20/400	20/100	20/30	20/30
"	10	Myopia	12/200	20/200	20/20	20/20
"	18	Cataracts-Surgical Aphakia	F. C.	F. C.	F. C.	20/40
"	58	Diabetic Retinitis-Cataract Surgical Aphakia	Nil	20/100	Nil	20/70
"	76	Nuclea Opacity-Surgical Aphakia	L. P.	20/100	L. P.	20/80
"	43	Cataract-Surgical Aphakia	20/400	L. P.	20/40	L. P.
"	64	Hyperopia	20/200	20/100	20/20	20/20
"	6	Hyperopia-Astigmatism	20/100	20/100	20/30	20/30
"	11	Hyperopia	20/200	20/200	20/25	20/25
"	13	Myopia	20/100	20/200	20/20	20/20
"	7	Myopia	20/400	20/400	20/30	20/30
"	65	Hyperopia-Nystagmus	20/400	20/400	20/20	20/20
"	78	Astigmatism	20/200	Nil	20/20	Nil
"	10	Astigmatism	20/200	20/200	20/40	20/40
"	8	Myopia	20/100	20/100	20/20	20/20
"	15	Myopia-Nystagmus	20/400	20/200	20/70	20/80
"	69	Astigmatism	Nil	20/100	Nil	20/25
"	7	Astigmatism	20/400	20/400	20/40	20/40
"	12	Astigmatism	20/200	20/200	20/40	20/40
Edgecombe	54	Senile Cataract-Surgical Aphakia	Nil	20/100	Nil	20/40
"	81	Senile Cataract-Surgical Aphakia	F.C. 3ft.	F.C. 3ft.	20/100	20/30
"	12	Hyperopia	20/100	20/100	20/20	20/20
"	9	Myopia-Astigmatism	20/200	20/100	20/50	20/50
"	9	Myopia-Astigmatism	20/200	20/200	20/20	20/20
"	60	Senile Cataract-Surgical Aphakia	20/100	L. P.	20/30	L. P.
"	25	Hyperopia-Presbyopia	20/200	20/200	20/20	20/20
"	47	Incipient Cataracts	20/100	20/100	20/20	20/20
"	36	Hyperopia-Astigmatism	20/200	20/200	20/100	20/30
"	35	Glaucoma-Hyperopia	Nil	20/200	Nil	20/50
Forsyth	69	Myopia-Presbyopia	20/100	20/200	20/20	20/50
"	36	Ametropia	20/200	20/200	20/20	20/100
"	12	Myopia	20/400	20/300	20/20	20/20
"	48	Ametropia-Presbyopia	20/400	20/800	20/50	20/100
"	68	Ametropia	20/200	20/200	20/20	20/20
"	14	Nystagmus-Myopia	20/100	20/100	20/40	20/30
"	14	Keratoconus	20/200	20/200	20/40	20/40
"	14	Keratoconus	20/100	20/100	20/40	20/40
"	40	Keratoconus-Anophthalmus	20/800	Nil	20/50	Nil
"	68	Corneal Scar-Ametropia	20/100	F.C. 3ft.	20/40	F.C. 3ft.
"	12	Ametropia	20/100	20/100	20/20	20/20
"	11	Myopia-Astigmatism	20/240	20/240	20/30	20/30
"	14	Nystahmus-Myopia	20/100	20/100	20/40	20/40
"	40	Ametropia-Choriod Degeneration	20/100	F.C. 5ft.	20/30	F.C. 5ft.
"	74	Ametropia-Presbyopia	20/200	20/200	20/30	20/30
"	69	Ametropia	20/200	20/200	20/30	20/30
"	37	Ametropia	20/400	20/400	20/20	20/20
"	32	Keratoconus	20/800	Nil	20/50	Nil

County	Age	Diagnosis	Vision Before Medical Care Given		Vision After Medical Care Given	
			Right Eye	Left Eye	Right Eye	Left Eye
Forsyth	71	Ametropia-Cataracts-Surgical Aphakia	5/200	F.C. 2ft.	5/200	20/20
"	72	Surgical Aphakia	20/100	F.C. 3ft.	20/100	20/50
"	37	Ametropia	20/200	20/200	20/20	20/50
Franklin	32	Hyperopia	20/200	20/200	20/20	20/20
"	7	Hyperopia	20/100	20/100	20/20	20/20
"	35	Hyperopia	20/100	20/100	20/20	20/70
Gaston	53	Hyperopia	20/400	20/400	20/20	20/20
"	14	Astigmatism-Hyperopia	20/200	20/200	20/40	20/40
Gaston	69	Bilateral Cataracts-Surgical Aphakia	F.C. 3ft.	F.C. 4ft.	F.C. 3 ft.	20/30
"	74	Nuclear Cataracts-Surgical Aphakia	H. M.	F.C. 2ft.	20/30	F.C. 2 ft.
"	70	Cataracts-Surgical Aphakia	L. P.	F.C. 5ft.	L. P.	20/20
"	81	Cataracts-Surgical Aphakia	L. P.	20/400	20/40	20/40
"	70	Cataracts-Surgical Aphakia	L. P.	F.C. 5ft.	L. P.	20/20
"	67	Hyperopia-Presbyopia	20/100	20/400	20/20	20/40
"	66	Hyperopia-Presbyopia	20/200	20/200	20/40	20/40
"	70	Hyperopia-Presbyopia	20/400	20/400	20/30	20/30
"	73	Cataracts-Surgical-Aphakia	F.C. 5 ft.	20/200	F.C. 5 ft.	20/50
"	65	Myopia-Presbyopia	10/400	10/400	20/25	20/25
"	30	Myopia	20/100	Nil	20/40	Nil
Gates	41	Cataract-Surgical Aphakia	L. P.	20/200	L. P.	20/40
"	9	Hyperopia-Astigmatism	20/200	20/200	20/70	20/70
"	30	Myopia	20/100	20/100	20/20	20/20
"	82	Retinal Arterio-Sclerosis-Cataracts-Surgical Aphakia	5/200	L. P.	20/20	L. P.
"	80	Hyperopia-Presbyopia	20/100	20/100	20/50	20/50
"	64	Presbyopia	20/100	20/100	20/20	20/20
"	75	Myopia-Astigmatism	20/200	Nil	20/50	Nil
"	62	Hyperopia-Presbyopia	20/200	20/200	20/30	20/20
Graham	14	Myopia-Astigmatism	20/100	20/100	20/20	20/20
"	12	Myopia-Astigmatism	20/100	20/100	20/30	20/30
"	11	Myopia-Astigmatism	20/300	20/400	20/70	20/70
"	12	Myopia-Astigmatism	20/100	20/100	20/50	20/50
"	15	Myopia	20/100	20/100	20/20	20/20
"	13	Cataracts-Surgical Aphakia	20/200	20/200	20/70	20/50
Granville						
Greene	10	Myopia	20/200	20/200	20/15	20/15
"	8	Hyperopia	20/100	20/100	20/20	20/30
"	9	Hyperopia	20/100	20/100	20/30	20/40
"	8	Amblyopia-Squint-Myopia	20/100	20/100	20/80	20/100
"	13	Astigmatism-Myopia	20/100	20/100	20/20	20/20
"	26	Astigmatism-Hyperopia	10/200	10/200	20/25	20/25
Guilford	72	Cataract-Surgical Aphakia	0/200	20/200	0/200	20/50
"	12	Astigmatism	20/100	20/100	20/30	20/30
"	12	Astigmatism	20/100	20/100	20/30	20/30
"	7	Astigmatism	20/100	20/100	20/40	20/40
"	12	Myopia	20/100	20/100	20/20	20/20
"	7	Hyperopia-Convergent Squint	20/100	20/100	20/50	20/50
"	12	Myopia	20/100	20/100	20/20	20/20
"	12	Strabismus-Hyperopia	F.C. 4ft.	20/400	20/50	20/20
"	74	Cataracts-Surgical Aphakia	Nil	20/200	Nil	20/50
"	72	Hyperopia-Presbyopia	20/200	20/200	20/20	20/20
"	73	Presbyopia-Cataract-Surgical Aphakia	20/200	20/200	20/20	20/200

County	Age	Diagnosis	Vision Before Medical Care Given		Vision After Medical Care Given	
			Right Eye	Left Eye	Right Eye	Left Eye
Guilford	65	Myopia-Lenticular Opacity-Surgical Aphakia	F.C. 10ft.	F.C. 10ft.	20/60	20/60
"	67	Presbyopia-Hyperopia	20/100	20/100	20/20	20/25
"	58	Hyperopia	20/100	20/100	20/20	20/20
"	64	Surgical Aphakia	F.C. 1ft.	F.C. 1ft.	20/30	20/100
"	65	Hyperopia-Astigmatism	20/100	12/200	20/25	20/25
"	50	Hypertension-Presbyopia-Hyperopia	15/200	10/200	20/40	20/20
"	58	Cataract-Surgical Aphakia	F.C. 2ft.	L. P.	20/30	L. P.
"	69	Cataract-Surgical Aphakia	L. P.	20/300	L. P.	20/25
"	69	Presbyopia-Astigmatism	20/200	20/200	20/20	20/20
"	11	Hyperopia	20/100	20/100	20/70	20/70
"	68	Surgical Aphakia-Hyperopia Cataract	20/200	20/200	20/70	20/70
"	65	Presbyopia-Hyperopia	20/100	20/200	20/70	20/70
"	10	Hyperopia	20/200	20/200	20/20	20/20
"	12	Astigmatism	20/100	20/100	20/20	20/20
"	70	Cataract-Surgical Aphakia	10/200	10/200	20/70	20/70
"	48	Hyperopia	20/200	20/200	20/25	20/25
"	14	Hyperopia	15/200	15/200	20/25	20/25
"	11	Hyperopia	20/200	20/200	20/50	20/200
"	74	Presbyopia-Hyperopia	20/100	20/100	20/20	20/20
Halifax	60	Optic Nerve Atrophy-Hyperopia	Nil	20/100	Nil	20/50
"	12	Hyperopia	20/100	20/100	20/100	20/30
"	25	Hyperopia	10/200	10/200	20/70	20/70
Harnett	10	Myopia	20/200	20/200	20/20	20/20
Haywood	12	Hyperopia-Astigmatism	20/200	20/200	20/50	20/50
"	2	Marked Hyperopia	20/200	20/200	20/50	20/50
"	60	Senile Cataracts-Surgical Aphakia	F. C.	L. P.	F. C.	20/30
"	43	Nystagmus-Anisotropia	20/200	20/100	20/50	20/70
"	59	Retinal Detachment-Surgical Correction	20/200	Nil	20/60	F.C.4in.
"	24	Bilateral Keratoconus	F.C. 6ft.	F.C. 6ft.	20/30	20/30
"	7	Alternating Strabismus-Hyperopia	20/200	20/200	20/30	20/30
"	9	Hyperopia	20/100	20/100	20/15	20/15
"	9	Astigmatism	20/200	20/200	20/15	20/15
"	26	Hyperopia-Presbyopia	20/200	20/100	20/30	20/30
"	15	Myopia-Astigmatism	20/100	20/100	20/20	20/20
"	12	Hyperopia-Astigmatism	20/100	20/100	20/20	20/20
"	50	Myopia-Presbyopia	20/100	20/100	20/20	20/20
"	73	Presbyopia	20/100	20/100	20/20	20/20
"	62	Myopia-Presbyopia	Nil	20/100	Nil	20/40
Henderson	72	Hyperopia	20/100	20/200	20/70	20/100
"	52	Hyperopia	20/100	20/100	20/30	20/30
"	85	Cataracts-Surgical Aphakia	20/200	Nil	20/70	Nil
"	12	Astigmatism	20/100	20/100	20/50	20/40
"	67	Hyperopia	20/200	20/200	20/20	20/20
"	75	High Myopia	20/400	20/400	20/70	20/70
"	80	Cataract-High Myopia-Surgical Aphakia	F. C.	20/200	F. C.	20/70
"	67	Cataract-High Myopia-Surgical Aphakia	L. P.	20/400	L. P.	20/60
"	14	Myopia-Astigmatism	20/400	20/400	20/70	20/70
"	11	Myopia	20/400	20/400	20/70	20/70
"	48	Hyperopia	20/100	20/100	20/40	20/40
"	57	Hyperopia	20/400	20/400	20/70	20/70

County	Age	Diagnosis	Vision Before Medical Care Given		Vision After Medical Care Given	
			Right Eye	Left Eye	Right Eye	Left Eye
Henderson	12	Myopia-Astigmatism	20/100	20/100	20/40	20/40
"	73	Hyperopia	20/100	20/100	20/30	20/30
"	53	Hyperopia-Presbyopia	20/200	20/200	20/30	20/30
"	81	Myopia-Presbyopia	20/200	20/100	20/200	20/70
	76	Myopia-Presbyopia	20/400	20/400	20/70	20/70
	67	Hyperopia	20/200	20/200	20/30	20/30
	14	Myopia-Astigmatism	20/200	20/100	20/30	20/35
"	65	Hyperopia-Astigmatism-Chorioditis	20/200	F. C.	20/30	20/200
"	15	Myopia	20/100	20/100	20/30	20/30
Hertford	11	Hyperopia	20/100	20/100	20/70	20/70
"	72	Senile Cataract-Surgical Aphakia	F.C. 3ft.	F.C. 3ft.	F.C. 3ft.	20/50
"	15	Hypermetropia-Dislocated Lens	20/200	20/100	20/40	20/40
Hertford	53	Presbyopia	20/100	20/200	20/20	20/20
Hoke						
Hyde	59	Cataracts-Surgical Aphakia	L. P.	F. C.	L. P.	20/20
"	12	Convergent Squint-Hyperopia	20/100	20/200	20/40	20/100
Iredell	69	Myopia-Presbyopia	20/300	20/400	20/30	20/30
"	75	Surgical Aphakia-Posterior Synechie	20/200	F.C. 3ft.	20/50	20/50
"	64	Surgical Aphakia-Senile Cataract	F.C. 2ft.	L. P.	20/30	L. P.
"	61	Ametropia-Presbyopia	20/100	20/100	20/30	20/30
Jackson	38	Hyperopia	20/100	20/100	20/20	20/20
"	13	Hyperopia	20/100	20/100	20/20	20/20
Johnston	83	Cataracts-Surgical Aphakia	10/200	F.C. 2ft.	10/200	20/30
"	63	Surgical Aphakia	20/200	20/200	20/200	20/50
"	73	Pterygium-Hyperopia	20/100	10/200	20/50	20/100
"	70	Cataract-Surgical Aphakia	20/100	20/200	20/80	20/100
"	70	Cataract-Surgical Aphakia	F.C. 3ft.	H. M.	20/70	H. M.
Jones	14	Hyperopia-Astigmatism	L. P.	20/200	20/100	20/50
Lee	9	Hyperopia	20/100	20/200	20/20	20/20
"	10	Optic Atrophy-Hyperopia	F.C. 18ft.	20/100	20/100	20/50
"	54	Ametropia-Presbyopia	20/100	20/100	20/20	20/20
"	68	Ametropia-Presbyopia	10/200	10/200	20/20	20/30
"	69	Ametropia	20/100	20/100	20/20	20/20
"	70	Ametropia-Presbyopia	20/200	20/200	20/20	20/30
"	76	Cataract-Surgical Aphakia	Nil	L. P.	Nil	20/70
"	75	Arteric-Sclerosis-Hyperopia	20/200	20/200	20/70	20/70
"	16	Myopia	20/300	20/300	20/200	20/70
"	60	Hyperopia	20/200	20/200	20/30	20/30
"	77	Cataract-Surgical Aphakia Coloboma	Nil	20/100	L. P.	20/30
"	77	Bilateral Senile Cataracts-Surgical Aphakia	20/200	18/200	20/50	20/50
"	50	Hyperopia-Presbyopia	20/200	20/200	20/40	20/40
"	76	Bilateral Senile Cataracts-Surgical Aphakia	20/200	20/200	20/70	20/200
"	83	Nuclear Cataract-Surgical Aphakia	F.C. 10ft.	F.C. 10ft.	20/70	20/70
"	78	Bilateral Cataract-Surgical Aphakia	F.C. 10ft.	F.C. 10ft.	20/50	20/50
"	68	Cataracts-Presbyopia-Surgical Aphakia	20/100	20/200	20/50	20/70
Lenoir	71	Cataract-Surgical Aphakia	F.C. 3ft.	20/100	F.C. 3ft.	20/30
"	44	Myopia-Hyperopia	20/100	20/100	20/20	20/20
"	66	Cataract-Surgical Aphakia	L. P.	20/400	L. P.	20/60
"	64	Hyperopia-Presbyopia	20/400	20/400	20/20	20/20
"	11	Hyperopia-Optic Atrophy	Nil	20/200	Nil	20/25

County	Age	Diagnosis	Vision Before Medical Care Given		Vision After Medical Care Given	
			Right Eye	Left Eye	Right Eye	Left Eye
Lenoir	75	Myopia	20/200	20/200	20/70	20/70
"	12	Ptosis-Hyperopia	Nil	20/100	Nil	20/20
"	45	Optic Atrophy-Hyperopia-Presbyopia	20/400	20/400	20/40	20/400
"	77	Cataracts-Surgical Aphakia	Nil	20/200	Nil	20/70
"	81	Hyperopia	20/400	20/400	20/100	20/60
"	68	Cataracts-Surgical Aphakia	L. P.	20/400	L. P.	20/60
"	13	Hyperopia	20/100	20/100	20/30	20/25
"	75	Cataracts-Surgical Aphakia	L. P.	20/400	L. P.	20/40
Lincoln	67	Bilateral Cataracts-Surgical Aphakia	L. P.	L. P.	20/50	L. P.
Macon	43	Astigmatism-Presbyopia	20/100	20/200	20/30	20/30
"	80	Cataract-Surgical Aphakia	20/200	20/200	20/100	20/50
"	75	Ametropia-Hyperopia	20/200	20/200	20/20	20/20
"	47	Ametropia-Hyperopia-Presbyopia	10/200	10/200	20/20	20/20
"	12	Bilateral Ectopion-Myopia	20/100	20/100	20/70	20/70
"	38	Cataract-Chronic Glaucoma-Surgical Aphakia	F.C. 8ft.	F.C. 10ft.	20/50	20/20
"	27	Squint-Hypcropia	20/400	20/400	20/200	20/80
Madison	22	Strabismus-Myopia	C.F. 10ft.	C.F. 10ft.	20/50	20/50
Martin	29	Cataract-Surgical Aphakia	Nil	4/200	Nil	25/30
"	65	Presbyopia-Hyperopia	20/200	20/200	20/30	20/30
"	72	Presbyopia-Hyperopia	20/200	10/200	20/30	20/20
"	12	Nystagmus-Albinism-Hyperopia	20/200	20/200	20/70	20/70
"	11	Myopia	20/100	20/100	20/50	20/50
"	76	Cataracts-Surgical Aphakia	L.Proj.	L.Proj.	L.Proj.	20/50
McDowell	32	Surgical Aphakia	C.F. 3ft.	Nil	20/40	Nil
"	74	Corneal Scar-Pterygium-Hyperopia	20/200	C.F. 2ft.	20/50	C.F. 2ft.
"	11	Ametropia	20/100	20/100	25/20	20/20
"	73	Senile Cataract-Surgical Aphakia	6/200	C.F. 6in.	6/200	20/30
"	80	Incipient Cataract-Myopia	5/200	4/200	20/50	20/30
"	7	Hypermetropia	20/100	20/100	20/50	20/40
"	10	Myopia	20/800	20/800	20/60	20/60
Mecklenburg	55	Hyperopia	20/200	20/200	20/20	20/20
"	31	Astigmatism	20/100	20/200	20/20	20/20
"	10	Myopia	20/100	20/100	20/20	20/20
	76	Incipient Cataracts-Myopia	C.F. 4ft.	C.F. 2ft.	C.F. 4ft.	20/20
	63	Chronic Glaucoma-Myopia	Nil	L. P.	Nil	20/40
	14	Simple Myopia	20/100	20/200	20/25	20/20
	50	Hyperopia-Presbyopia	20/200	C. F.	20/20	20/25
	43	Myopia-Astigmatism-Presbyopia	20/100	20/200	20/20	20/200
	12	Hypermetropia	20/100	20/100	20/20	20/20
	45	Hypermetropia-Presbyopia	20/100	20/100	20/20	20/20
	50	Myopia-Astigmatism-Presbyopia	20/100	20/200	20/30	20/20
	11	Myopia	12/200	12/200	20/20	20/20
	12	Myopia	20/200	20/200	20/20	20/20
	7	Myopia	20/200	20/200	20/20	20/20
	45	Hyperopia-Astigmatism-Presbyopia	20/200	20/200	20/30	20/30
	34	Cataracts-Surgical Aphakia	3/200	10/200	20/80	20/100
	10	Nystagmus-Hyperopia	20/100	20/100	20/80	20/80
	14	Congenital Nystagmus-Myopia	20/100	20/100	20/120	20/80
	13	Myopia	20/200	20/200	20/25	20/25
	15	Myopia	20/100	20/200	20/25	20/25
	63	Myopia-Presbyopia	L.P	8/200	20/20	8/200
	15	Traumatic Cataracts-Surgical Aphakia	20/200	L. P.	20/45	L. P.

County	Age	Diagnosis	Vision Before Medical Care Given		Vision After Medical Care Given	
			Right Eye	Left Eye	Right Eye	Left Eye
Mecklenburg	6S	Surgical Aphakia	C.F. 5ft.	C.F. 4ft.	20/50	20/50
"	52	Incipient Cataracts-Myopia	L. P.	20/200	20/50	20/200
"	56	Senile Cataracts-Surgical Aphakia	20/200	20/300	20/30	20/300
..	14	Myopia-Astigmatism	20/100	20/100	20/30	20/40
	.64	Cataract-Surgical Aphakia	Light	6/200	Light	20/50
..	44	Presbyopia-Hyperopia	20/200	20/200	20/40	20/40
	64	Presbyopia-Myopia	20/100	20/200	20/20	20/20
..	40	Myopia-Presbyopia	20/200	20/100	20/20	20/20
	57	Hyperopia-Presbyopia	20/100	20/100	20/20	20/20
..	71	Myopia-Presbyopia	20/200	20/200	20/200	20/50
"	13	Myopia-Astigmatism	20/200	20/100	20/50	20/200
..	50	Presbyopia-Astigmatism	20/200	20/200	20/40	20/30
	49	Hyperopia-Presbyopia	20/200	20/200	20/30	20/70
	.55	Presbyopia	20/200	20/100	20/20	20/20
..	82	Chronic Dacrocystitis-Myopia	C.F. 5ft.	C.F. 10ft.	20/40	20/40
"	71	Hyperopia-Presbyopia	20/200	20/200	20/25	20/25
	62	Myopia-Presbyopia-Cataract Surgical Aphakia	L. P.	8/200	L. P.	20/40
"	9	Hypermetropia	20/200	20/100	20/20	20/20
	7	Hyperopia	20/100	20/100	20/50	20/50
	43	Hypermetropia-Presbyopia	20/200	20/200	20/20	20/20
	46	Hyperopia-Astigmatism	20/200	20/200	20/30	20/30
..	36	Hypermature Cataract-Surgical Aphakia	20/200	L. P.	20/200	20/20
Mitchell	9	Hyperopia-Astigmatism	20/100	20/100	20/20	20/20
"	10	Hyperopia-Astigmatism	20/100	20/100	20/50	20/50
"	9	Hyperopic Astigmatism	20/100	20/200	20/50	20/200
	77	Hyperopia Astigmatism	20/200	20/200	20/30	20/100
"	10	Hyperopic Astigmatism	20/100	20/100	20/40	20/50
"	11	Hypermetropia-Astigmatism	Nil	20/100	Nil	20/20
Montgomery	79	Senile Cataract-Hyperopia	20/100	20/200	20/100	20/30
"	56	Bilateral Cataracts-Surgical Aphakia	20/100	L. P.	20/100	20/40
"	77	Senile Cataracts-Surgical Aphakia	20/200	20/200	20/20	20/200
'	6	Astigmatism	20/100	20/100	20/40	20/40
	54	Cataracts-Surgical Aphakia	L P	L. P.	20/30	L. P.
Moore	65	Senile Cataracts-Surgical Aphakia	5/100	5/100	20/70	20/70
"	10	Amblyopia-Hyperopia	20/100	20/200	20/30	20/100
"	49	Hyperopic Astigmatism	20/200	20/200	20/20	20/20
"	15	Myopic Astigmatism	20/100	20/100	20/40	20/50
"	85	Cataracts-Surgical Aphakia	Nil	20/100	Nil	20/40
"	52	Opaque Cornea-Surgical Aphakia	Nil	20/400	Nil	20/40
"	73	Presbyopia-Hyperopia	20/200	15/200	20/30	20/45
'	62	Cataracts-Surgical Aphakia	C.F 3ft.	Nil	20/50	Nil
.'	72	Bilateral Cataracts-Surgical Aphakia	C.F.	Nil	20/20	Nil
"	52	Hyperopia-Presbyopia	20/100	20/100	20/30	20/30
"	56	Surgical Aphakia	20/200	20/100	20/200	20/30
"	73	Hyperopia-Presbyopia	20/100	20/200	20/30	20/30
"	72	Hyperopia	20/100	20/100	20/20	20/20
"	75	Incipient Cataracts-Hyperopia	C.F. 10ft.	C.F. 10ft.	20/70	20/70
"	23	Cataracts-Surgical Aphapia	C.F. 3ft.	C.F. 3ft.	C.F. 8ft.	20/70
"	63	Cataracts-Surgical Aphapia	20/100	20/200	20/40	20/40
Nash	23	Myopic Astigmatism	20/100	Nil	20/30	Nil
"	11	Esotropia-Chorio-Retinitis-Astigmatism	H. M.	20/200	H. M.	20/70
New Hanover	15	Cataracts-Surgical Aphapia	L. P.	Nil	20/70	Nil

County	Age	Diagnosis	Vision Before Medical Care Given		Vision After Medical Care Given	
			Right Eye	Left Eye	Right Eye	Left Eye
New Hanover.	46	Cornea & Conjunctiva burned-Hyperopia.	20/200	20/200	20/100	20/70
"	67	Senile Cataracts-Surgical Aphakia ..	20/400	20/400	20/70	20/100
Northampton	22	Astigmatism.	20/100	20/100	20/20	20/20
"	24	Hyperopia..........	20/200	20/200	20/20	20/20
Onslow........	8	Astigmatism.... ...	20/200	20/200	20/50	20/50
"	68	Myopia-Cataracts..................	20/400	20/800	20/200	20/70
"	13	Myopia....	15/100	15/100	20/20	20/15
"	59	Surgical Aphapia.	L. P.	20/400	20/30	20/400
Orange	10	Hyperopic Astigmatism.......	20/100	20/100	20/40	20/40
"	58	Cataract-Optic Atrophy-Surgical Aphakia........	L. P.	C. F.	L. P.	20/40
Pamlico	69	Surgical Aphapia.....	H. M.	20/200	H.M.	20/70
"	71	Presbyopia-Hyperopia.....	20/400	20/400	20/30	20/30
"	67	Corneal Scar-Presbyopia-Myopia.......	L. P.	20/200	L. P.	20/25
Pasquotank	54	Cataract-Surgical Aphakia...............	20/200	20/200	20/40	20/50
"	77	Cataract-Surgical Aphakia...............	20/100	L. P.	20/60	L. P.
"	58	Surgical Aphakia....	Nil	3/200	Nil	20/60
"	79	Hyperopia-Presbyopia.......	10/200	10/200	20/30	20/70
"	38	Myopic Astigmatism.	5/200	5/200	20/60	20/60
Pender........	9	Hyperopia....	20/100	20/100	20/50	20/50
"	8	Myopia.............................	20/200	20/200	20/70	20/100
"	13	Hyperopia.......	20/100	20/100	20/20	20/50
"	8	Hyperopia....	20/100	20/100	20/40	20/40
"	10	Hyperopia.............................	20/100	20/100	20/50	20/50
Perquimans..................						
Person....	8	Astigmatism	20/100	20/100	20/70	20/100
Pitt..............................	8	Astigmatism....	20/400	20/400	20/40	20/40
"	72	Cataract-Surgical Aphakia.	20/400	20/100	20/400	20/40
"	70	Presbyopia-Hyperopia......	20/200	20/200	20/50	20/50
"	68	Hyperopia	20/200	20/200	20/50	20/200
"	65	Cataracts-Surgical Aphakia	Nil	20/200	Nil	20/20
"	11	Ametropia....	20/200	20/200	20/40	20/40
"	70	Cataracts-Surgical Aphakia.	L. P.	L. P.	20/25	L. P.
"	88	Cataracts-Surgical Aphakia............. ..	20/400	20/400	20/400	20/80
"	79	Astigmatism-Presbyopia.	20/200	20/200	20/70	20/70
"	16	Ametropia....	20/100	20/200	20/20	20/20
"	72	Incipient Cataracts-Myopia........	20/200	20/200	20/50	20/100
"	40	Myopic Astigmatism.....	20/100	20/100	20/20	20/20
"	65	Hyperopia-Presbyopia....	20/100	20/200	20/20	20/25
"	14	Myopia........	20/200	20/200	20/60	20/60
"	8	Traumatic Cataract-Surgical Aphakia............................	20/100	Nil	20/30	Nil
"	62	Presbyopia-Hyperopia...................... .....:	20/100	20/100	20/20	20/20
"	68	Astigmatism-Presbyopia.......	20/100	20/100	20/25	20/25
"	39	Myopia............................	10/200	20/100	20/70	20/70
"	8	Hyperopia.......................	20/100	20/100	20/70	20/70
"	76	Surgical Aphakia	C.F. 2ft.	L. P.	20/25	L. P.
"	44	Astigmatism....	20/200	20/200	20/30	20/20
"	13	Astigmatism.	20/100	20/100	20/20	20/20
"	10	Astigmatism.....................	20/200	20/200	20/20	20/20
"	10	Hyperopia.......................	20/400	20/200	20/70	20/20
"	50	Astigmatism-Presbyopia....	20/100	20/100	20/30	20/30
"	70	Astigmatism-Presbyopia................	20/100	20/100	20/20	20/20
"	79	Astigmatism-Presbyopia-Pterygium..	20/200	20/100	20/70	20/70

County	Age	Diagnosis	Vision Before Medical Care Given		Vision After Medical Care Given	
			Right Eye	Left Eye	Right Eye	Left Eye
Pitt	69	Incipient Cataracts-Hyperopia	20/200	20/200	20/70	20/70
"	68	Cataracts-Surgical Aphakia	20/200	Nil	20/20	Nil
"	9	Astigmatism	20/100	20/100	20/20	20/20
"	73	Myopia	20/200	20/200	20/40	20/40
"	65	Hyperopia	20/200	20/200	20/30	20/30
"	75	Myopia	10/200	10/200	20/70	20/70
"	52	Incipient Cataracts-Hyperopia	Nil	20/100	Nil	20/40
"	74	Surgical Aphakia-Cataract	5/400	L. P.	20/20	L. P.
"	69	Leukoma-Cataract-Surgical Aphakia	20/300	20/100	20/300	20/60
"	77	Astigmatism-Presbyopia	20/400	20/400	20/25	20/20
"	78	Myopia-Cataracts	5/400	5/400	20/40	20/40
"	70	Opacities-Surgical Aphakia	20/200	20/200	20/40	20/50
"	76	Cataract-Trauma-Surgical Aphakia	L. P.	20/400	L.P.	20/40
"	69	Cataract-Presbyopia	20/400	20/400	20/400	20/40
"	80	Astigmatism-Cataracts	20/200	20/400	20/50	20/400
"	14	Hyperopia-Astigmatism	20/400	20/400	20/400	20/40
"	11	Astigmatism	20/400	20/400	20/30	20/30
"	14	Hyperopia-Astigmatism	20/200	20/200	20/40	20/40
"	50	Myopia-Astigmatism-Hyperopia	20/200	20/200	20/20	20/20
"	88	Presbyopia-Hyperopia	20/400	20/400	20/30	20/30
Polk	17	Cataract-Surgical Aphakia	20/200	L. P.	20/20	20/30
"	16	Myopia	20/400	20/400	20/40	20/30
"	55	Hyperopia	20/200	20/200	20/70	20/70
"	77	Optic Atrophy-Myopia	20/200	20/400	20/60	20/100
"	55	Chorio-Retinitis-Myopia	20/200	20/200	20/70	20/70
"	13	Hyperopic Astigmatism	20/100	20/100	20/00	20/00
"	11	Myopic Astigmatism	20/100	20/100	20/35	20/50
"	6	Hyperopia Astigmatism	20/100	20/100	20/30	20/30
"	9	Hyperopia Astigmatism	20/100	20/100	20/40	20/40
"	15	Myopia	20/400	20/400	20/20	20/20
"	13	Myopia Astigmatism	20/200	20/200	20/30	20/30
"	13	Myopic Astigmatism	20/200	20/200	20/40	20/40
"	16	Myopia	20/200	20/200	20/40	20/100
"	11	Myopic Astigmatism	20/100	20/100	20/40	20/40
"	13	Myopic Astigmatism	20/200	20/200	20/30	20/30
"	10	Hyperopia Astigmatism	20/100	20/100	20/30	20/30
Randolph	14	Myopia	20/100	20/100	20/30	20/20
"	14	Myopia	20/100	60/100	20/20	20/20
"	15	Myopia	20/100	20/100	20/20	20/20
Richmond	10	Hyperopia-Anisometropia	20/100	20/100	20/20	20/40
"	11	Compound Myopic Astigmatism	20/100	20/200	20/50	20/50
"	11	Hyperopic Astigmatism	20/100	20/100	20/50	20/40
"	14	Exotorpia-Alternating-Hyperopia	20/200	20/100	20/70	20/40
"	75	Cataracts-Surgical Aphakia	H. M.	CF. 1 ft.	5/25	C.F. 1 ft.
"	54	Surgical Aphakia-Cataracts	C.F. 1t.	5/200	20/30	5/200
"	13	Myopia	20/200	20/200	20/20	20/20
"	7	Esotropia	20/100	20/200	20/20	20/20
"	49	Retinal-Arterio-Sclerosis-Hyperopia	20/100	20/100	20/30	20/30
"	78	Hyperopia-Astigmatism	20/200	20/100	20/20	20/20
"	74	Hyperopia Astigmatism	1/200	5/200	20/20	20/30
"	51	Hypertension-Hyperopia	10/200	20/200	20/50	20/40
"	73	Hyperopia-Presbyopia	20/200	20/200	20/25	20/25
"	72	Hyperopia-Myopia-Pterygium	20/200	10/200	20/50	20/50
"	83	Senile Cataract-Myopia	C.F. 6ft.	20/200	20/40	20/40

County	Age	Diagnosis	Vsion Before Medical Care Given		Vision After Medical Care Given	
			Right Eye	Left Eye	Right Eye	Left Eye
Richmond	75	Senile Cataract-Surgical Aphakia	H. M.	C.F. 1ft.	20/25	C.F. 1ft.
"	10	Hyperopia-Squint	20/200	20/100	20/60	20/40
"	71	Hyperopic Astigmatism	20/100	20/200	20/50	20/50
"	70	Incipient Cataracts-Hyperopia	7/100	10/200	20/70	20/70
"	83	Surgical Aphakia-Cataract	3/200	15/200	20/50	10/200
"	65	Pterygium-Myopia	20/200	20/200	20/50	20/50
"	95	Incipient Cataract-Myopia	L. P.	20/100	L. P.	20/70
"	46	Cataract-Myopia	15/200	L. P.	20/70	L. P.
Robeson	67	Myopia	20/200	20/200	20/20	20/40
"	68	Cataract-Surgical Aphakia	C.F. 3ft.	C.F. 4ft.	20/30	C.F. 4ft.
"	67	Cataract-Surgical Aphakia	C.F. 2ft.	C.F. 2ft.	C.F. 2ft.	20/50
"	64	Pterygium-Hyperopia	20/100	L. P.	20/50	L. P.
"	9	Hyperopia	5/200	20/100	5/200	20/25
"	11	Hyperopia	20/200	20/100	20/60	20/30
"	78	Myopia-Incipient Cataracts	10/200	12/200	20/40	20/40
"	12	Hyperopic Astigmatism	20/100	20/100	20/30	20/30
"	76	Presbyopia-Myopia	20/100	20/20	20/30	20/30
"	56	Cataract-Presbyopia-Hyperopia	Nil	20/100	Nil	20/30
"	11	Hyperopia Amblyopia	20/200	20/200	20/90	20/90
"	22	Myopia	15/200	15/200	20/80	20/80
"	69	Hyperopia-Presbyopia	20/200	20/400	20/20	20/20
"	73	Hyperopia-Presbyopia	20/200	20/200	20/30	20/30
"	66	Lenticular changes-Myopia	20/300	20/300	20/30	20/30
Robeson	76	Hyperopia-Presbyopia	10/200	20/200	20/50	20/50
"	80	Hyperopia-Presbyopia	15/200	15/200	20/50	20/50
"	76	Hyperopia-Astigmatism	20/400	20/400	20/30	20/50
"	72	Hyperopia-Presbyopia	20/400	20/400	20/25	20/80
"	74	Hyperopia-Presbyopia	20/100	20/300	20/40	20/25
"	8	Hyperopia Strabismus	20/100	20/100	20/40	20/40
"	13	Hyperopia	20/200	20/400	20/80	20/100
"	46	Hyperopia	20/400	20/400	20/25	20/25
"	74	Myopia-Opacities	20/200	20/100	20/200	20/60
"	53	Hyperopia-Presbyopia	20/400	20/400	20/60	20/60
"	74	Leukoma-Hyperopia-Astigmatism	20/100	20/100	20/25	20/100
"	80	Myopia	20/100	20/200	20/50	20/50
"	75	Myopia-Astigmatism	20/200	Nil	20/40	Nil
"	72	Astigmatism	20/400	20/100	20/70	20/25
"	58	Hyperopia-Presbyopia	20/200	20/100	20/40	20/30
Rockingham	68	Senile Cataract-Surgical Aphakia	C.F. 6ft.	L. P.	20/30	L. P.
"	10	Ametropia-Myopia	20/100	20/100	20/50	20/50
"	75	Ametropia-Leukoma	L. P.	20/100	L. P.	20/30
"	75	Senile Cataracts-Surgical Aphakia	H. M.	C.F. 1ft.	20/25	C.F. 1ft.
"	73	Presbyopia-Astigmatism	20/100	20/100	20/30	20/30
"	72	Cataracts-Surgical Aphakia	L. P.	C.F. 5ft.	L. P.	20/20
Rowan	38	Bilateral Mature Cataracts-Surgical Aphakia	20/800	H.M.	20/800	20/20
"	84	Senile Cataracts-Surgical Aphakia	20/200	L. P.	20/30	L. P.
"	11	Myopia	20/100	20/100	20/20	20/20
"	72	Hyperopia-Presbyopia	20/200	20/200	20/40	20/40
Rutherford	10	Hyperopia-Astigmatism	20/200	20/200	20/70	20/70
"	9	Hyperopia	20/100	20/100	20/50	20/40
"	9	Myopia	20/100	20/100	20/20	20/20
"	12	Hyperopia	20/100	20/100	20/40	20/40
"	9	Hyperopia	20/100	20/100	20/20	20/30
"	10	Hyperopia	20/200	20/200	20/40	20/40

County	Age	Diagnosis	Vision Before Medical Care Given		Vision After Medical Care Given	
			Right Eye	Left Eye	Right Eye	Left Eye
Rutherford	13	Hyperopia	20/200	20/200	20/40	20/40
"	49	Hyperopia-Astigmatism	20/200	20/200	20/20	20/20
"	9	Hyperopia-Astigmatism	20/100	20/100	20/20	20/20
"	9	Myopia Astigmatism	20/1C0	20/100	20/30	20/30
"	72	Cataract-Surgical Aphakia	C.F. 3ft.	L. P.	20/40	L. P.
	64	Traumatic Cataract-Surgical Aphakia	Nil	20/200	Nil	20/70
"	66	Ametropia	20/100	20/200	20/30	20/40
"	13	Myopic-Astigmatism	20/200	20/200	20/30	20/70
	60	Hyperopic Astigmatism	20/200	10/200	20/20	20/20
"	7	Hyperopia	20/200	20/100	20/30	20/20
"	30	Hyperopia	20/200	20/200	20/30	20/30
"	58	Hyperopia	20/200	20/100	20/20	20/20
: "	14	Bilateral-Optic Atrophy-Hyperopia	20/200	20/200	20/70	20/50
"	10	Myopic Astigmatism	20/100	20/100	20/40	20/40
	7	Hyperopic Astigmatism	20/100	20/100	20/50	20/50
"	8	Hyperopic Astigmatism	20/200	20/200	20/70	20/70
"	9	Hyperopic Astigmatism	20/100	20/100	20/50	20/50
"	40	Hyperopic Astigmatism	20/200	20/200	20/20	20/20
::	12	Myopia	20/200	20/200	20/30	20/30
	10	Hyperopia	20/200	20/100	20/20	20/20
	14	Hyperopia	20/100	20/100	20/35	20/20
	11	Hyperopia	20/1C0	20/100	20/40	20/40
"	11	Hyperopic Astigmatism	20/100	20/100	20/40	20/40
"	11	Hyperopic Astigmatism	20/100	20/100	20/40	20/40
"	8	Hyperopia-Astigmatism	20/200	20/200	20/40	20/40
	13	Myopia	20/100	20/100	20/100	20/60
	14	Bilateral Optical Atrophy-Hyperopia	20/200	20/200	20/70	20/50
	79	Incipient Cataract-Myopia	20/200	20/100	20/200	20/40
	16	Coloboma-Astigmatism	C.F. 6ft.	C.F: 6ft.	20/50	20/70
	67	Pterygium-Myopia	C. F.	20/100	C. F.	20/30
	75	Cataract-Surgical Aphakia	20/400	C.F. 4ft.	20/30	C.F. 4 ft.
"	55	Hyperopia-Cataract-Surgical Aphakia	20/100	20/100	20/50	20/40
	70	Cataract-Myopia	20/200	20/400	20/50	20/200
"	76	Myopia	20/200	20/200	20/200	20/40
	77	Myopia	20/100	20/100	20/70	20/70
	53	Hyperopia-Presbyopia	20/300	20/300	20/25	20/25
	65	Cataracts-Surgical Aphakia	C.F. 5ft.	C.F. 5ft.	20/30	C.F. 5 ft.
	10	Hyperopia	20/100	20/100	20/50	20/50
	70	Hyperopia-Presbyopia	20/200	20/400	20/60	20/400
"	80	Hyperopic Astigmatism	20/200	20/200	20/50	20/70
"	78	Cataract	20/40	C.F. 3ft.	20/70	C.F. 3 ft.
"	69	Arteriosclerotic Degeneration-Hyp.	20/300	20/100	20/70	20/70
Sampson	75	Cataract-Surgical Aphakia	20/400	C.F. 4ft.	20/30	C.F. 4 ft.
"	55	Hyperopia-Cataract	20/100	20/100	20/50	20/40
"	70	Cataracts-Myopia	20/200	20/400	20/50	20/200
: "	76	Cataract-Surgical Aphakia	L. P.	L. P.	20/200	20/40
	77	Retinal Degeneration-Hyperopia	20/100	20/100	20/70	20/70
	53	Hyperopia-Presbyopia	20/300	20/300	20/25	20/25
"	65	Cataracts-Surgical Aphakia	C.F. 5ft.	C.F. 5ft.	20/30	C.F. 5 ft.
	10	Hyperopia	20/100	20/100	20/50	20/50
"	70	Hyperopia-Presbyopia	20/200	20/400	20/60	20/400
	80	Hyperopic Astigmatism	20/200	20/200	20/50	20/70

County	Age	Diagnosis	Vision Before Medical Care Given		Vision After Medical Care Given	
			Right Eye	Left Eye	Right Eye	Left Eye
Sampson	78	Cataract-Surgical Aphakia	20/400	C.F. 3ft.	20/70	C.F. 3ft.
"	69	Arteriosclerotic Degeneration-Myopia	20/300	20/400	20/70	20/70
Stanly	12	Myopia	20/300	20/400	20/35	20/400
"	82	Old Choroiditis-Hyperopia-Astigmatism	20/400	20/300	20/400	20/40
'	63	Hyperopia-Presbyopia	20/100	20/100	20/20	20/20
'	34	Hyperopia-Pterygium	20/200	20/200	20/30	20/30
"	69	Cataracts-Hyperopia-Astigmatism	20/400	20/400	20/80	20/100
"	12	Myopia	20/300	20/400	20/35	20/400
Stokes	67	Chronic Conjunctivitis-Keratitis	C.F 10ft.	C.F. 10ft.	20/40	20/30
"	10	Chalazion-Myopia	20/200	20/200	20/20	20/20
"	81	Ametropia-Presbyopia	20/400	20/400	20/50	20/100
"	11	Ametropia-Amblyopia	20/200	20/300	20/50	20/100
"	40	Nystagmus Congenital-Hyperopia	20/100	20/100	20/50	20/70
"	75	Bilateral Incipient Cataracts-Myopia	20/100	20/100	20/50	20/30
"	74	Hyperopia	20/200	Nil	20/50	Nil
Surry	13	Hyperopia	20/100	20/100	20/20	20/20
"	13	Hyperopia	20/200	20/200	20/20	20/20
"	13	Keratitis	20/100	20/200	20/20	20/20
"	36	Astigmatism	20/100	20/100	20/40	20/40
"	9	Hyperopia	20/200	20/200	20/20	20/20
"	10	Astigmatism	20/100	20/100	20/30	20/30
"	8	Hyperopic-Astigmatism	20/100	20/200	20/30	20/30
"	13	Astigmatism-Albinism	20/100	20/100	20/100	20/70
"	13	Congenital-Ptosis-Hyperopia	20/200	20/200	20/200	20/70
Surry	75	Incipient Cataracts-Myopia	C.F. 15ft.	C.F. 7ft	20/40	20/70
"	6	Ametropia	20/100	20/100	20/30	20/30
"	10	Ametropia	20/200	20/200	20/50	20/50
"	50	Concomitant Internal Strabismus-Hyperopia	20/100	20/100	20/50	20/30
"	11	Ametropia-Myopia	20/200	20/100	20/30	20/20
"	82	Bilateral Senile Cataract-Hyperopia	L. P.	20/800	20/50	20/800
"	13	Myopia	20/100	C.F. 3ft.	20/50	20/50
"	65	Ametropia	20/400	20/400	20/50	20/50
Swain	16	Hyperopia	20/100	20/100	20/40	20/40
"	67	Macula Degeneration-Myopia	20/100	10/200	20/50	20/200
"	17	Hyperopia	20/100	20/100	20/20	20/20
"	4	Myopia-Exophoria	10/200	10/200	20/30	20/20
"	22	Hyperopia-Presbyopia	20/100	20/200	20/20	20/20
"	76	Cataracts-Astigmatism	C. F.	C. F.	20/60	C.F.
"	47	Myopia-Presbyopia	20/200	20/100	20/20	20/20
"	74	Cataracts-Surgical Aphakia	20/100	20/200	20/50	20/50
"	67	Cataract-Surgical Aphakia	20/200	20/200	20/70	20/30
"	87	Cataract-Surgical Aphakia	20/200	L. P.	20/70	20/30
"	44	Ametropia-Hyperopia	20/200	5/200	20/20	5/200
Transylvania	70	Cataract-Surgical Aphakia	H. M.	20/200	H. M.	20/25
Tyrrell	50	Hyperopia-Presbyopia	20/100	20/100	20/30	20/30
Union	67	Cataract-Surgical Aphakia	C.F. 2ft.	C.F. 2ft.	20/25	20/40
"	67	Hyperopia	20/200	20/200	20/20	20/40
"	50	Hyperopia	20/200	20/200	20/40	20/40
"	8	Hyperopia	20/100	20/100	20/20	20/50
"	30	Hyperopia	20/100	20/100	20/30	20/20
"	8	Hyperopia	20/200	20/200	20/40	20/30
"	17	Hyperopia	15/200	15/200	20/40	20/40

County	Age	Diagnosis	Vision Before Medical Care Given		Vision After Medical Care Given	
			Right Eye	Left Eye	Right Eye	Left Eye
Union	26	Hyperopia	20/200	20/200	20/50	20/40
"	75	Cataract-Surgical Aphakia	20/200	20/200	20/200	20/30
"	16	Myopia	10/200	10/200	20/70	20/70
"	79	Cataract-Surgical Aphakia	Nil	20/100	Nil	20/30
"	12	Myopia	20/100	20/100	20/20	20/20
"	75	Cataract-Surgical Aphakia	C.F. 2ft.	20/200	20/20	20/200
"	15	Myopic-Astigmatism	20/100	20/100	20/30	20/20
"	7	Hyperopia	20/200	20/200	20/30	20/30
"	7	Hyperopia	20/200	20/200	20/30	20/30
"	12	Hyperopia-Astigmatism	20/100	20/200	20/20	20/20
"	13	Hyperopia	15/200	15/200	20/50	20/50
"	86	Cataracts-Myopia-Astigmatism	20/200	20/200	20/100	20/50
"	12	Hyperopic Astigmatism	20/200	20/200	20/30	20/30
"	69	Hyperopic Astigmatism	20/200	20/200	20/30	20/30
"	14	Hyperopic Astigmatism	20/200	20/100	20/30	20/30
Vance	68	Hyperopic Astigmatism	20/100	20/100	20/30	20/30
"	8	Hyperopia	20/100	20/100	20/50	20/50
"	14	Myopia-Astigmatism	20/100	20/100	20/30	20/30
"	7	Cataracts-Surgical Aphakia	20/100	20/100	20/20	20/20
"	72	Cataracts-Myopia	L. P.	L. P.	20/70	L. P.
"	53	Cataracts-Myopia	L. P.	L. P.	L. P.	20/50
"	66	Myopia	20/200	20/200	20/40	20/30
Wake	71	Myopia	10/200	10/200	20/40	20/30
"	74	Myopia	10/200	20/200	20/40	20/40
"	24	Hyperopia	C.F. 1ft.	C.F. 1ft.	20/50	20/100
"	22	Myopia-Astigmatism	20/200	20/200	20/40	20/50
"	54	Hyperopia	20/100	20/100	20/20	20/20
"	16	Myopia	20/200	20/200	20/20	20/20
"	13	Myopia	20/200	20/100	20/20	20/20
"	10	Myopia-Astigmatism	20/200	20/200	20/30	20/30
"	10	Myopia	20/200	20/100	20/20	20/20
"	79	Myopia	20/100	20/200	20/30	20/200
"	65	Atrophic Globe-Hyperopia	Blind	20/100	Nil	20/30
"	15	Myopia	20/100	20/200	20/20	20/20
"	63	Hyperopia	18/200	20/200	20/30	20/30
"	65	Cataract-Hyperopia	Nil	20/200	Nil	20/50
"	65	Surgical Aphakia	20/400	20/200	20/40	20/200
"	74	Macular Degeneration-Myopia	F.C. 4ft.	20/100	F.C. 4ft.	20/50
"	37	Acute Iritis-Conjunctivitis	L. P.	L. P.	20/100	20/30
"	14	Myopia-Astigmatism	20/100	20/100	20/40	20/40
"	38	Myopia	20/100	20/100	20/30	20/30
"	67	Hyperopia-Astigmatism	20/400	20/100	20/20	20/20
"	7	Myopia	20/100	20/100	20/20	20/20
"	75	Myopia-Presbyopia	20/100	20/100	20/40	20/40
"	79	Surgical Aphakia-Cataract	L. P.	L. P.	L. P.	20/20
"	11	Hyperopia-Astigmatism	20/200	6/200	20/40	20/70
"	28	Myopia-Astigmatism	20/200	20/200	20/70	20/70
"	9	Hyperopia-Astigmatism	20/200	20/200	20/40	20/40
"	68	Cataracts-Astigmatism	20/200	20/100	20/100	20/40
"	72	Cataracts-Astigmatism	C.F. 3ft.	20/200	20/70	20/200
"	40	Hyperopic Astigmatism	20/100	20/100	20/30	20/30
"	13	Congenital Hyperopia	20/200	20/200	20/20	20/20
"	75	Hyperopia-Presbyopia	20/200	20/200	200/30	20/30
"	74	Hazy Lenses-Hyperopia	20/200	20/200	20/70	20/70
"	9	Albinism-Amblyopia-Myopia	20/200	20/200	20/70	20/70

County	Age	Diagnosis	Vision Before Medical Care Given		Vision After Medical Care Given	
			Right Eye	Left Eye	Right Eye	Left Eye
Vance	68	Cataracts-Surgical Aphakia	C.F. 3ft.	C.F. 3ft.	20/30	C.F. 3ft.
"	79	Bilateral Immature Cataracts-Hyperopia	20/100	20/100	20/30	20/40
"	68	Hyperopia-Presbyopia	10/200	20/100	20/100	20/50
"	6	Hyperopia-Astigmatism	20/200	20/200	20/20	20/20
"	9	Hyperopia-Astigmatism	4/200	8/200	20/20	20/20
"	65	Hyperopia-Astigmatism	20/100	20/100	20/20	20/20
"	7	Myopia-Astigmatism	1/200	2/200	20/50	20/50
"	67	Hyperopia-Astigmatism	20/100	20/100	20/20	20/20
"	13	Myopia	20/200	20/200	20/20	20/20
"	12	Hyperopia-Astigmatism	20/200	20/200	20/20	20/70
"	11	Hyperopia-Astigmatism	20/100	20/200	20/20	20/100
"	15	Myopia-Exotropia	20/200	20/200	20/20	20/100
"	65	Optic Atrophy-Myopia	Nil	20/200	Nil	20/40
Warren	10	Progressive Myopia	20/200	20/200	20/50	20/50
Watauga	8	Hyperopia	20/100	20/100	20/20	20/20
"	12	Amblyopia-Ametropia	10/100	15/200	20/50	20/50
"	11	Hyperopia	12/200	12/200	20/50	20/50
"	8	Myopia	20/200	5/200	20/40	20/200
"	10	Myopia	16/200°	16/200	20/20	20/20
"	13	Myopia	16/200	20/200	20/70	20/70
"	58	Hyperopia-Astigmatism	10/200	20/200	20/30	20/30
"	10	Hyperopia-Astigmatism	20/100	20/100	20/40	20/40
"	56	Presbyopia-Hyperopia	20/100	20/100	20/30	20/30
"	44	Presbyopia-Hyperopia	20/200	20/200	20/50	20/50
Wayne	61	Conjunctivitis	20/100	20/200	20/20	20/25
"	7	Refractive error-Hyperopia	20/400	20/400	20/40	20/40
"	11	Myopia-error of Refraction	20/200	20/200	20/30	20/30
Wilkes	32	Myopia-Astigmatism	20/100	20/100	20/30	20/30
"	13	Myopia	10/400	10/400	20/60	20/60
"	71	Hyperopia	20/200	20/200	20/20	20/20
"	49	Hyperopia	20/100	20/100	20/20	20/20
"	51	Hyperopia	20/200	20/200	20/20	20/20
"	45	Hyperopia	20/200	20/200	20/20	20/20
"	51	Hyperopia	20/200	20/200	20/40	20/50
"	76	Hyperopia	20/100	20/100	20/20	20/20
"	67	Glaucoma-Hyperopia	20/100	Nil	20/70	Nil
"	73	Myopia-Macular Degeneration	2/200	3/200	2/200	20/50
"	56	Retinal Arteriosclerosis-Myopia	20/200	20/100	20/30	20/40
"	74	Surgical Aphakia	20/200	L. P.	20/50	H.M.
"	30	Cataract-Iris Atrophy-Hyperopia	H.M.	20/200	H. M.	20/70
"	60	Hyperopia	2/200	2/200	20/30	20/30
"	59	Hyperopia	20/200	20/100	20/20	20/20
"	65	Cataract-Corneal Scar-Aphakia	2/200	2/200	20/70	20/70
"	78	Cataract-Hyperopia	Nil	2/200	Nil	20/70
"	11	Myopia	20/200	20/200	20/50	20/40
"	11	Hyperopia-Astigmatism	20/200	20/200	20/20	20/20
"	43	Hyperopia	20/100	20/200	20/20	20/20
"	9	Hyperopia	20/100	20/200	20/40	20/40
"	10	Myopia	20/200	20/200	20/20	20/50
"	63	Hyperopia	20/400	20/200	20/20	20/20
"	64	Cataract-Surgical Aphakia	20/100	20/200	20/30	20/70
"	14	Ametropia	20/100	20/200	20/20	20/20
"	15	Ametropia	20/100	2/200	20/40	20/50
Wilson	15	Hyperopia	20/100	20/100	20/20	20/20

County	Age	Diagnosis	Vision Before Medical Care Given		Vision After Medical Care Given	
			Right Eye	Left Eye	Right Eye	Left Eye
Wilson	9	Hyperopia	20/100	20/100	20/20	20/20
"	14	Hyperopia	20/200	20/100	20/20	20/20
"	7	Hyperopia-Astigmatism	20/100	20/100	20/40	20/40
'	10	Hyperopia-Astigmatism	20/200	20/200	20/70	20/70
"	8	Hyperopia-Astigmatism	20/200	20/200	20/30	20/30
"	12	Hyperopia-Astigmatism	20/300	20/100	20/70	20/20
"	10	Hyperopia-Astigmatism	20/200	20/100	20/70	20/70
'	19	Myopia-Astigmatism	20/100	20/100	20/20	20/20
"	15	Hyperopia-Astigmatism	20/100	20/100	20/20	20/20
'	25	Hyperopia-Astigmatism	20/400	20/400	20/30	20/30
"	6	Hyperopia	20/200	20/200	20/20	20/20
"	5	Hyperopia	20/400	20/400	20/40	20/40
"	10	Hyperopia	20/100	20/100	20/20	20/20
"	67	Cataract-Myopia	2/200	2/200	20/40	20/50
"	11	Hyperopia-Astigmatism	20/100	20/100	20/20	20/20
"	14	Hyperopia-Astigmatism	10/200	10/200	20/30	20/30
'	12	Hyperopia-Astigmatism	10/200	20/200	20/70	20/50
"	12	Hyperopia-Astigmatism	20/200	20/200	20/40	20/40
'	11	Hyperopia-Astigmatism	20/100	20/100	20/20	20/20
'	12	Hyperopia	20/100	20/100	20/20	20/20
"	40	Hyperopia	20/400	20/200	20/20	20/20
"	14	Hyperopia	20/400	20/200	20/70	20/70
"	58	Cataract-Surgical Aphakia	H. M.	20/200	H. M.	20/30
Yadkin	29	Keratitis	20/200	20/200	20/20	20/20
"	65	Ametropia	20/200	20/200	20/20	20/20
"	54	Ametropia	20/100	20/100	20/20	20/20
'	10	Astigmatism	20/200	20/100	20/20	20/20
"	17	Hyperopia	10/200	8/200	20/39	20/30
'	18	Ametropia	20/100	20/100	20/20	20/20
"	41	Ametropia	20/100	20/100	20/30	20/30
"	7	Myopia	20/200	20/100	20/30	20/30
"	10	Ametropia	20/200	20/200	20/20	20/20
Yancey	11	Subluxation fo lens-Hyperopia	20/100	20/100	20/40	20/40
"	53	Hyperopia-Astigmatism	20/100	20/100	20/20	20/20
"	18	Myopia	20/200	20/200	20/15	20/15

APPENDIX II

Data on the 14,083 indigent persons examined by Ophthalmologists during the past biennium.

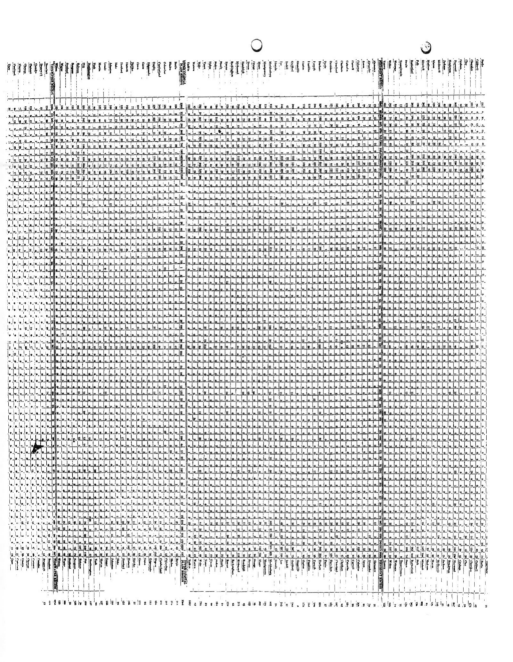

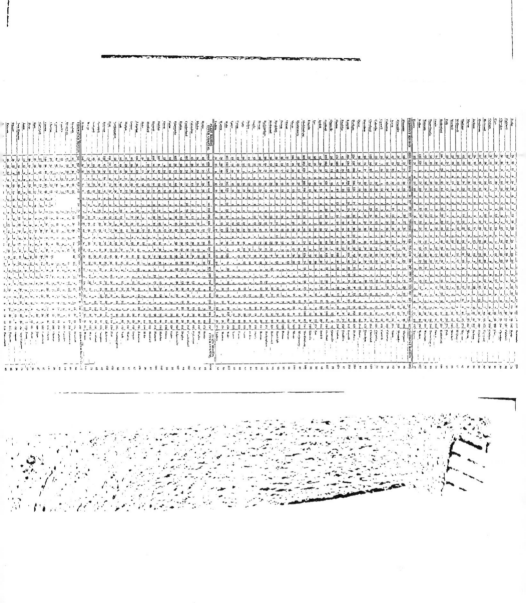

EXPENDITURES FOR 1944-45 AND 1945-46

CHAPTER 53, PUBLIC LAWS OF 1935, CODE 326

Providing funds for conservation and restoration of sight, occupational rehabilitation and placement, special case work services, and miscellaneous services to the blind.

*Purposes and/or Objects	Expenditures for 1944-45	Expenditures for 1945-46
I. ADMINISTRATION		
101. Salary Executive Secretary	$ 3,240.00	$ 3,820.00
102. Salaries and Wages Staff	3,425.33	4,165.00
103. Expense of Commission	359.42	360.00
104. Supplies and Materials	35.00	100.00
105. Postage Tel. and Tel.	600.00	600.00
106. Travel Expense	1,016.60	1,029.23
107. Printing and Binding	402.86	265.00
108. General Expense	29.57	30.00
109. Insurance and Bonding	13.75	10.50
110. Equipment	86.49	97.58
TOTAL	$ 9,209.02	$ 10,477.31
II. DIRECT AID TO NEEDY BLIND RESTORATION & CONSERVATION OF VISION		
201. Salaries and Wages	$ 2,910.00	$ 5,091.21
202. Supplies and Materials	40.00	39.05
203. Medical Appliances	14,007.00	14,922.08
204. Travel Expense	1,390.04	2,605.19
205. Printing and Binding	19.74	19.08
206. Examination and Operation	21,662.97	22,723.33
207. Sight Saving Teachers		
TOTAL	$ 40,029.75	$ 45,399.94
III. PLACEMENT SERVICE FOR THE BLIND		
301. Salaries and Wages	$ 4,430.02	$ 5,556.82
302. Supplies and Materials	35.00	35.00
303. Travel Expense	1,200.00	1,197.38
304. Equipment	96.24	70.25
IV. DIRECT AID TO NEEDY BLIND, TRAINING AND EMPLOYMENT		
401. Salaries and Wages	$ 4,938.20	$ 4,500.00
402. Supplies and Materials	425.00	635.16

* The items in this report follow the wording of the State Budget for 1945-46 to facilitate comparisons with 1944-45.

403.	Printing and Binding	15.00	
404.	Training Service	8,149.60	7,932.91
405.	Equipment	8,535.36	13,823.15
406.	Trucks		745.00
407.	Medical Examinations		550.00
408.	Corrective Surgery		500.00
409.	Hospitalization		850.00
410.	Transportation	1,231.20	295.31
411.	Prosthetic Devices		499.52
412.	Maintenance		16,360.54
	TOTAL	$ 23,294.36	$ 46,691.59

V. ADMINISTRATIVE SERVICE TO AID
    BLIND RECIPIENTS

501.	Salaries	$ 2,680.00	$ 3,320.00
	TOTAL	$ 2,680	$ 3,320.00

VI. SALARY INCREASE

VII. PRE-CONDITIONING CENTER FOR
     ADULT BLIND $ 14,990.14

     TOTAL $ 14,990.14

VIII. EMERGENCY SALARIES

	EMERGENCY SALARIES	$ 2,776.68	$ 1,857.20
	TOTAL REQUIREMENTS	83,751.07	129,595.63
	LESS: ESTIMATED RECEIPTS		
1.	Miscellaneous	3,515.16	7,121.05
2.	Federal Administration	5,524.62	4,603.60
3.	Glasses	13,697.55	14,690.92
	TOTAL	$ 22,737.33	$ 26,415.57
	APPROPRIATIONS	$ 61,013.74	$103,180.06

PUBLIC LAW 113, 1943, VOCATIONAL REHABILITATION
FEDERAL CODE 2804

I. ADMINISTRATION

101	Salary and Wages	$ 5,448.66	$ 8,141.37
102	Travel	736.65	1,361.59
103	Postage	606.78	815.69
104	Supplies	364.45	100.94
105	Printing and Binding	272.08	147.85
106	Rent	900.00	900.00

*Purposes and/or Objects	Expenditures for 1944-45	Expenditures for 1945-46
107 Repairs and Alterations	64.42	17.33
108 Office Equipment	766.46	507.56
109 Expense of Board Members Bureau of Employment for Blind	55.45	40.30
110 Exp. of Advisory Medical Comm.	......	......
111. Retirement System	203.07	334.45
112 Part-time Consulting Ophthalmologist	600.00	600.00
113 Special Salary Bonus	709.83	542.43
Total	$ 10,727.85	$ 13,509.51

II. VOCATIONAL GUIDANCE & PLACEMENT SERVICES

	Expenditures for 1944-45	Expenditures for 1945-46
201 Salary and Wages	22,467.70	40,746.92
202 Travel	16,962.13	21,875.53
203 Postage, Tel. and Tel.	....	415.38
204 Supplies	......	355.49
205 Office Equipment	2,978.24	1,094.44
206 Repairs and Alterations	....	144.81
207 Transportation of Clients	....	263.32
208 Retirement System	902.24	1,595.16
209 Special Salary Bonus	2,318.41	2,274.25
Total	$ 45,628.72	$ 68,765.30

III. CASE SERVICES (Other than War-Disabled Civilians)

	Expenditures for 1944-45	Expenditures for 1945-46
301. Examinations	$ 282.00	$ 200.00
302. Treatment	1,719.75	1,467.70
303. Prosthetic Devices	1,093.47	311.15
304. Hospitalization	1,596.39	760.55
305. Transportation	626.22	505.23
306. Maintenance	27,851.84	16,871.46
307. Training	22,402.93	25,665.99
308. Training—Supplies and Materials	1,302.49	347.16
309. Equipment	6,735.23	5,107.09
TOTAL	$ 63,610.32	$ 51,236.33

IV. CASE SERVICES (War-Disabled Civilians)

401. Examinations	......	......
402. Prosthetic Devices	......	......

* The items in this report follow the wording of the State Budget for 1945-46 to facilitate comparisons with 1944-45.

*Purposes and/or Objects	Expenditures for 1944-45	Expenditures for 1945-46
403. Training		
404. Training Supplies and Materials	.	
405. Maintenance		
406. Transportation	.	
407 Equipment		
TOTAL		
TOTAL REQUIREMENTS	$119,966.89	$133,511.14
ESTIMATED RECEIPTS:		
Balance July 1, 1945 .	$ 1,909.50	$ 1,001.92
Federal Receipts	119,059.31	150,654.41
TOTAL ESTIMATED RECEIPTS	$120,968.81	$151,656.33

CHAPTER 124, PUBLIC LAWS OF 1937, CODE 610

Providing payments and direct relief grants to needy blind.

I. ADMINISTRATION

		Expenditures for 1944-45	Expenditures for 1945-46
101.	Salaries and Wages	$ 11,330.00	$ 15,103.91
102.	Supplies and Materials -	240.00	335.87
103.	Postage and Tel. and Tel.	600.00	600.00
104.	Travel Expense	4,772.40	4,553.47
105.	Printing and binding	149.85	50.00
106.	Repairs and Alterations	77.98	72.60
107.	Insurance and Bonding		
108.	Equipment	192.36	185.32
109.	Medical Certification	400.00	400.00
110.	Exp. of Advisory Medical Comm.		
	TOTAL	$ 17,762.59	$ 21,301.17

II. PAYMENTS TO NEEDY BLIND

201.	State	$118,533.43	$147,845.91
202.	Federal	262,791.13	310,951.15
203.	County	118,446.43	145,848.41
	TOTAL	$499,770.99	$604,645.47

III. COUNTY EQUALIZATION FUND $ 10,000.00 $ 10,000.00

* The items in this report follow the wording of the State Budget for 1945-46 to facilitate comparisons with 1944-45.

*Purposes and/or Objects	Expenditures for 1944-45	Expenditures for 1945-46
IV. COUNTY ADMINISTRATION		
401. Salaries and Wages	$ 27,161.05	$ 37,520.49
402. Travel Expense	20,203.79	22,116.79
403. Federal Administration Direct to Counties	11,395.40	11,008.45
TOTAL	$ 58,760.24	$ 70,645.73
V. SALARY INCREASE		
VI. EMERGENCY SALARIES	$ 4,791.14	$ 3,637.39
TOTAL REQUIREMENTS	$591,084.96	$710,229.76
LESS: ESTIMATED RECEIPTS		
1. Federal Aid to Blind	$262,791.13	$310,951.15
2. Federal Administration	39,882.52	55,009.77
3. County Aid to the Blind	138,377.15	173,673.96
4. Miscellaneous	4,167.16	4,594.88
5. Federal Funds		
TOTAL	$445,217.96	$544,229.76
APPROPRIATION	$145,867.00	$166,000.00

* The items in this report follow the wording of the State Budget for 1945-46 to facilitate comparisons with 1944-45.

CPSIA information can be obtained
at www.ICGtesting.com
Printed in the USA
BVHW04*1046170918
527708BV00015B/1896/P